PENGU

1971

Rachna Bisht Rawat is the author of six books published by Penguin Random House India, including the bestsellers *The Brave* and *Kargil*. She lives in Gurugram with Hukum the bright-eyed, bushy-tailed golden retriever; an eclectic collection of books and music; and Manoj Rawat, the man in Olive Green who met her when he was a gentleman cadet at the Indian Military Academy and offered to be her comrade for life. Occasionally, they are visited by Saransh the Wise, who has moved out to explore the world on his own. She can be reached at www.rachnabisht.com and rachnabisht@gmail.com. Her Instagram handle is @rachna_bishtrawat.

ADVANCE PRAISE FOR THE BOOK

'In this exciting book, Rachna takes you to the front lines—blood-curdling, gory battles with khukris and guns; Su-7s and Maruts in strike missions; a Naval diver leading Mukti *yoddhas* behind enemy lines; and much more. There are extraordinary acts of dedication, gallantry and emotions seen only among soldiers in the very thick of battle. Each story leaves you with goosebumps and admiration. With her realistic descriptions, sensitive human touch and exclusive art of story-weaving, Rachna has taken war-story narration to a very high level'—General V.P. Malik, PVSM, AVSM, ADC, former chief of the army staff

'As the distance between the extraordinary generation of soldiers that fought the third Indo–Pak war and a generation that struggles to remember it widens, Rachna Bisht Rawat unearths stories of the strange bonds that war forges in her book *1971*. She tells them with a sense of urgency, given that the men who fought it are now in the evening of their lives, reconstructing some of the well-known and not-so-well-known battles in riveting fashion. But it is the stories of the prisoners of war—their loves, loss and the sense of no closure as time ticks—that Rachna tells both poetically and poignantly'—Deepa Alexander, *The Hindu*

1971
CHARGE OF THE GORKHAS
and Other Stories

RACHNA BISHT RAWAT
Bestselling author of *The Brave* and *Kargil*

PENGUIN
VEER
An imprint of Penguin Random House

PENGUIN VEER

USA | Canada | UK | Ireland | Australia
New Zealand | India | South Africa | China

Penguin Veer is part of the Penguin Random House group of companies whose addresses can be found at global.penguinrandomhouse.com

Published by Penguin Random House India Pvt. Ltd
4th Floor, Capital Tower 1, MG Road,
Gurugram 122 002, Haryana, India

First published in Penguin Veer by Penguin Random House India 2021

10 9 8 7 6 5 4 3

The views and opinions expressed in this book are the author's own and the facts are as reported by her which have been verified to the extent possible, and the publishers are not in any way liable for the same. Nothing in this book is intended to cause offence or hurt the sentiments of any individual, community, section of people, group or religion.

ISBN 9780143454366

Typeset in Bembo Std by Manipal Technologies Limited, Manipal
Printed at Thomson Press India Ltd, New Delhi

www.penguin.co.in

For all those men in uniform who smiled and stepped into DMS boots, battlefields, fighter planes and war ships, forgetting that they were fathers, sons and husbands too

For those who returned and those who never could

For those who are now stardust, and for those who stare blankly out of prison cells in foreign lands

For all our soldiers—the martyrs, the missing and the living

Your sacrifice shall never be forgotten

For my friend Renu Agal, who introduced me to the beautiful world of book-writing but didn't stay back to see where that journey would take me

In 1970, general elections were held in Pakistan which led to the Awami League, helmed by Sheikh Mujibur Rahman, securing an absolute majority in East Pakistan and insisting upon autonomy. The rulers of West Pakistan responded with a military crackdown. A terrible genocide was launched against the Bengali people. It is estimated that around 3 million people were killed. Rape, torture, conflicts followed, due to which approximately 10 million people fled the country, seeking refuge across the border, which put India under a huge economic burden.

India supported the Mukti Bahini—an army of freedom fighters—in their fight for liberation and demanded that Pakistan create conditions for the return of the refugees to their homes. On the evening of 3 December 1971, Pakistan Air Force attacked the Indian airfields of Srinagar, Avantipur, Pathankot, Uttarlai, Jodhpur, Ambala and Agra. The strikes were perfectly timed with a full-moon night for maximum visibility and were carried out on a Friday, which would surprise India since Muslims consider it a sabbath.

Prime Minister Indira Gandhi went on air a little after midnight and made a historic address to the nation. Calling the air strikes a 'declaration of war against India', she said, 'Aggression must be met, and the people of India will meet it, with fortitude and determination, and with discipline and utmost unity.'

The thirteen-day military conflict, also known as the Bangladesh Liberation War, was one of the shortest wars in history. It ended with a decisive win for India and led to the creation of Bangladesh. On 16 December 1971, the Eastern Command chief of the Pakistan Army, Lt Gen. A.A.K. Niazi, signed the instrument of surrender and, along with 93,000 troops, surrendered to the joint forces of Indian Army and Bangladesh's Mukti Bahini. It was the largest military surrender after World War II. East Pakistan became Bangladesh, with Awami League leader Sheikh Mujibur Rahman becoming its first President in January 1972.

The Simla Agreement was signed by Indira Gandhi and Zulfikar Ali Bhutto, President of Pakistan, at the midnight of 2 July 1972. India agreed to return all 93,000 Pakistani POWs. It is extremely unfortunate that it did not negotiate the return of those Indian soldiers who had gone 'missing in action', many of whom could never come back home again.

India suffered more than 12,000 casualties in the 1971 war; 2908 men laid down their lives for the country.

Contents

Foreword

Rachna Bisht Rawat has done it again! Her latest book, *1971: Charge of the Gorkhas and Other Stories*, sears one's senses with mind-boggling stories of the heroics of soldiers, sailors and airmen of the Indian armed forces during the Indo–Pak war of 1971.

Rachna's stories have a life of their own. In my opinion, there is no author in India or abroad who has the ability to pack so much emotion in stories about war, the effect it has on the protagonists and on those they leave behind. Her deep research, her eye for detail, her understanding of the minds of the soldier and the efforts she has made to track down veterans who have a story to tell across the length and breadth of India, have resulted in this collection of unforgettable stories.

My advice to the reader is to read the stories 'one sip at a time', so that they can be better savoured. Her stories are better remembered because all of them do not have happy endings. Each story has a pathos of its own, bringing to the reader the reality of war and its aftermath.

The main story, 'Charge of the Gorkhas', is a fantastic account of the last khukri attack in modern military history carried out by the 4th Battalion of the 5th Gorkha Rifles (FF). It is about the amazing courage and leadership of the battalion's commanding officer, Lieutenant Colonel Arun Harolikar, as well as the gallant officers and men that he led into a difficult operation and yet came out on top. The aggressive and remorseless use of the khukri in this attack made a deep impact on the psyche of the Pakistani soldiers who were at the receiving end of cold steel and who, thereafter, were extremely reluctant to get into close combat with the Gorkhas in the subsequent battles that followed.

But let me not say too much. I need to let the reader savour the magic of these stories told by an amazing storyteller. This book commemorates a war that made India a major power in the region and should be read by every citizen of India and the world.

New Delhi Major General Ian Cardozo,
November 2021 AVSM, SM

Introduction

When military histories are written, they paint men in uniform as fearless braves ready to kill and die for their country. Sacrifice is glorified and martyrdom revered. No one tells us what was going on inside the young soldier's head and heart when the bugle called. When I started writing *1971*, I knew I was going to focus on the human stories that traditional war histories tend to leave out, and that is what I have tried to do in this book.

In these pages you will find stories of phenomenal courage, but you will also meet men who felt terrible fear, regret and trauma. You will meet soldiers who were scared, who were weak, who were facing internal conflict, and yet they chose to go ahead and do what they believed was right. For me, they were heroes too.

'Charge of the Gorkhas', my main story, is about the gutsy warriors of 4/5 Gorkha Rifles who attack an enemy position, fortified by machine guns, with naked *khukris* in their hands and the war cry of '*Jai Mahakali! Aayo Gorkhali*' on their lips. When I sent my final draft to Col M.M. Malik (eighty), who had fought in that battle, he shot back an email saying the story took him back to 1971 and filled him with so much *josh* that he was ready to pack his field bag and go to the battlefield once again to launch a fresh attack against any enemy soldiers still hanging around there. Col Y.S. Rawat (eighty-one), who lost a leg in the war, told me he had no regrets and, if given a chance, would be happy to fight for his country once again, even if it meant losing his other leg.

'Bloodied in Tangail' is about a young wannabe paratrooper who has never been on a plane but stubbornly insists on going for an attack with his unit, which is going to be airdropped behind enemy lines. 'A Box of Sweets' is the story of a Sikh officer who faces a moral dilemma when a grievously injured Pakistani prisoner of war asks to be set free so that he can go back to tend to his sick child. 'Behind Enemy Lines' is the tale of a naval diver who is so enraged by the atrocities inflicted on helpless Bengalis that he decides to cross the border, against orders, risking death and court martial.

The story closest to my heart is 'Missing'. It is about a brave young fighter pilot who went missing when his plane crashed inside Pakistan. The hero of that story, for me, is his young wife, who continued to believe for many years that he was alive and has spent the last fifty years of her life trying to find out what happened to him. When I marvelled at her fortitude, she smiled and told me, 'For the establishment, he is just a file. For me, he is the husband I love. *Agar unke liye main nahi karungi toh kaun karega* (If I don't do this for him, who will)?'

That story is a reminder that for every soldier who returned home from the battlefield, there was a comrade who never did. I sincerely hope that telling these stories will contribute to keeping their memories alive. Because soldiers don't die on battlefields; they die only when an ungrateful nation forgets their sacrifice. Remembrance is all that we can offer them in return for what they did.

Missing

5 December 1971
Amritsar airport
Around 1230 hours

Flight Lieutenant Vijay Vasant Tambay is walking purposefully down the tarmac in his blue overalls. For a moment, his mind goes back to Ambala, where he has left Damayanti, his wife of eighteen months. He knows she hates being alone and would be ticking days off the calendar till he returns. Her response to his '*Aaj tumne ghar mein kya kiya*?' has always been '*Intezaar*!' Tambay smiles to himself.

It is a clear day and the winter sun is nearly blinding. Helmet clasped in the crook of his arm, he squints to look at his faithful Su-7, tail number B-839, that waits for him, fully armed and ready for action. A bright-eyed airman in a crew cut, not older than twenty, is standing near the stepladder. He steps forward to take Tambay's helmet that has his nickname, 'Uncle', painted on it. Taking a cursory walk around the aircraft to check if everything is in order, Tambay climbs into the open cockpit and, strapping himself into the narrow seat, puts on his headset and helmet. He pushes the lever that slides the glass canopy cover of the cockpit into place and, after asking Air Traffic Control for permission to fly, signals a thumbs up to the airman.

Snapping to attention, the airman salutes Tambay as per the mandatory procedure followed across the world every time a combat aircraft lifts off. That launch salute is not just a sign of respect but also a traditional final goodbye in case the pilot never returns. Tambay salutes back. It is destined to be his last flight.

Adjusting the mission route map on the instrument panel coaming, Tambay pushes the throttle forward. The jet engine revs up, and the mighty Su-7 starts to taxi out to the runway. The white taxi line is zipping past as the aircraft starts to move, and he can hear his own breath on the headset. He sees his mission leader, Squadron Leader (later Air Marshal) V.K. Bhatia, call sign Eagle 1, entering the runway. Bhatia opens full power and moves forward. Tambay follows just 100 m behind. The two Su-7s roll down the runway faster and faster. Tambay watches Bhatia lift off smoothly and follows him up in the air. The two planes turn and, with a frightening roar, cross the international border at a speed of 900 km per hour, taking barely two minutes to travel the 22 km distance. Flying at a height of about 100 m, they have to pull up to avoid the high-tension pylons as they cross the border south of Lahore. They are heading towards Shorkot Road. Their mission is to strike the enemy airfield and the planes parked there.

The two Su-7s hit Shorkot Road around 1345 hours. Lunchtime has deliberately been chosen for the mission since enemy aircraft defences are expected to be down. However, the pilots soon realize that this is a mistaken belief. The airfield is dotted with more than a hundred lethal anti-aircraft ack-ack guns waiting for the Indian fighters, who had already caused much damage the day before. The two Su-7s lose no time in making an attack. They engage the target successfully and then reverse and come back for a second strike. As Tambay pulls up and dives down to strafe the airfield, his plane comes under heavy fire. He hears the rattling sound of shells meeting fuselage and feels a sudden jerk.

Looking in the rearview mirror, he notices a spiralling plume of smoke curling out of his aircraft and realizes he has been hit. The Su-7 immediately starts losing height. Much as he tries, Tambay cannot pull the aircraft up. He is fiddling desperately with the controls but his efforts are futile. The grey smoke cloud is getting denser. He can now see fumes outside his window too. His worried eyes move to the controls. Altitude has started to drop. On his radio telephony (RT) set he can hear his leader saying, 'Tambay, eject.' And then again, much louder, his voice raised in concern and urgency, 'Tambay! Eject!' The call is repeated multiple times. Tambay does not answer. His aircraft has gone into a steep dive.

Blinded by tears of rage and sorrow, a shattered Bhatia dives down and unleashes his rockets at the target. He then turns around and flies back to Amritsar alone. Tambay's plane crashes on the runway, engulfing the area in a huge ball of fire. The time is 1350 hours.

~

August 2021
Munirka Vihar
Delhi

'*Paal le ik rog nadan zindagi ke vaaste*
sirf sehat ke sahare umr to kat ti nahin.'

Frail, grey-haired and neatly dressed in a white salwar kameez and dupatta, seventy-two-year-old Damayanti Vijay Tambay leans back in her easy chair and recites these lines to me. It has been fifty years since her fighter pilot husband left the house looking affectionately into her eyes with an '*Aata hun*'. She is still waiting.

Finding out what happened to him is the *rog* of her life, she says. 'It is my *fitoor*, my obsession, it gives meaning to my life.' I see no frustration or helplessness in her eyes. Just sadness and steely resolve. Her courage is no less than her husband's, who went to fight for his country.

The day Flt Lt Vijay Tambay's plane crashed, twenty-two-year-old Damayanti was sitting alone at home. The previous night had been traumatic. She had spent most of it standing in the deep, moist, ant-infested trench that had been dug out in front of the house as a bomb shelter. In her pocket was a steel spoon and a thick roll of cotton. Tambay had told her that bomb attacks often jammed the jaws of victims, and keeping something between the teeth could prevent that. 'Air-raid sirens pierced the silence of the night, ack-ack guns boomed, and I just stood there trembling with cold and fear,' she remembers. In the afternoon, some air force personnel rang the doorbell. Not mentioning the crash, they told her that it might be best if she went back home to stay with her parents. 'I thought maybe Vijay wanted that, so I packed my suitcase, locked up the house and walked down to the railway station that was about 2 km from my house.' Boarding the Kalka Mail, which made a two-minute stop at Ambala, Damayanti spent the night in the first-class corridor because no one wanted to open their coupe for her. When some passengers got down at Delhi the next morning, she got a place to sit and eventually reached Allahabad, where her parents lived.

On the night of 6 December, she was absent-mindedly fiddling with the radio when suddenly her blood froze. Radio Pakistan was announcing the names of Indian prisoners of war (POWs). Flt Lt Tambay was one of the names called out.

On 8 December, a telegram arrived, confirming the news that he was missing in action. It was from the Indian government. 'Very selfishly, my first emotion was of relief. I thought he would not have to fight any more. And since his name had been publicly announced by Pakistan, I believed he would be repatriated. The thought that he might never come back just did not cross my mind,' says Damayanti.

While both the Indian Air Force and the Pakistan Air Force appear to believe that Tambay did not survive the crash, Damayanti feels her husband baled out of his burning aircraft and was taken prisoner. She starts to tell me why, but I want to know Vijay Vasant Tambay better, so I implore her to start from that breezy winter morning in Delhi when a dashing fighter pilot drove into her life in a green Fiat car and swept her off her feet. 'A bottle-green Fiat,' she corrects me gently and, with an endearing smile, goes on to describe the eighteen-month romance that has sustained her for a lifetime.

~

February 1970
Maharashtra Sadan
New Delhi

A delicately built twenty-two-year-old, with large, long-lashed eyes, is fiddling nervously with her badminton racquet. The reigning national badminton champion, Damayanti is in Delhi to play a tournament. She normally travels alone but this time her parents—her lawyer father and school principal mother—are accompanying her to meet a boy whose matrimonial proposal has come for her. He is a fighter pilot—the twenty-seven-year-old son of Vasant Tambay, an officer from the first batch of the Indian Administrative Service presently posted as secretary to the Maharashtra government. The families meet. 'Vijay had driven down from Ambala. His father told us to go out and spend some time together,' Damayanti remembers. She says she was shell-shocked when the chivalrous air force officer stepped forward and opened the car door for her. At her incredulous query, '*Gadi ka darwaza hamare liye kab tak khologe*?', he smiled and answered, '*Sari umar.*'

Since neither has any idea about Delhi, they decide to go and check the location of the Railway Stadium where she is to play her match in the evening. But the hall is locked and they decide to go to Connaught Place, where they sit in a quaint little garden café that used to be where Palika Bazaar is these days. They have coffee under a garden umbrella, both wondering '*Kya baat karein*'. 'He was more organized then than I am even now,' Damayanti remembers. 'He had made a list of things he wanted to share with me, like his date of birth, details of siblings, hobbies, etc. So he told me all that and asked me about myself.'

She says she liked him immediately but wondered if he would want to marry her since she thought she had very simple looks. 'We were ordinary middle-class people, *us time mein make-up karna, ye sab tha nahi*. I was prepared *ki mujhe toh mana hi kar denge.*' She was surprised to find that he appeared equally smitten by her. The alliance was fixed and both sets of parents departed the next day, leaving the two young people to spend a day together. Damayanti says she was so proud of her precious new possession—her fiancé—that she even took him to meet a friend's mother. 'I wanted to show him off to someone. *Mujhe laga, Mummy Daddy ke alawa kisi aur ko bhi toh dikhaun*,' she says. 'He came along willingly and then dropped me off at the railway station and drove off to Ambala.'

Damayanti and Vijay got married two months later, and she moved to Ambala, though much of her time was still spent travelling for practice sessions and matches. 'He would often joke with his colleagues that "my wife has come on casual leave; she will go back soon",' she remembers. 'When I offered to give up playing badminton, he said no. "*Ek baar hamare naam se bhi toh jeeto.*"' Damayanti did win her third national title as Damayanti Vijay Tambay, but when she was given the prestigious Arjuna Award in 1972, delayed by a year because of the war, he was no longer around to take pride in her achievement.

~

Air Marshal Bhatia remembers Flt Lt Tambay as a close friend, one of the pilots he had trained and his comrade-in-war who had been with him in all three missions to bomb Shorkot Road (two on day one and one on day two). 'He was lively, full of beans, a brilliant singer and used to love singing that song from *Padosan*, "Ek Chatur Naar". He would sing it with great panache, mimicking the accents perfectly,' he smiles.

For Damayanti, Vijay was an affectionate, responsible, loving husband. 'He would come back home from work and when I asked him about office, he would say, "*Wo choro. Tum batao, tumne kya kiya sara din*?" I would get irritated and answer, "*Intezaar kiya, aur kya kiya.*" He would want to know if I had eaten and if I hadn't he would tell me, "*Khana kha lena chahiye tha.*" *Mujhe shikayat thi unko gussa kyun nahi aata.* I too had nothing to be angry about. *Koi baat milti hi nahi thi aisi.*'

'Professionally, he was very sound, very patriotic and completely dedicated to his job. He had trained in America for a year and in Russia for six months and was considered a very good pilot,' she adds.

~

3 December 1971
1750 hours
Ambala

War clouds had been looming, and the Indian Air Force had been on alert since November. The fighter pilots of 32 Squadron, whose home base was Ambala, had been moved to Amritsar, which was their operational airbase. On 3 December, some of them—including Sqn Ldr Bhatia and Flt Lt Tambay—had come back to Ambala for a turnaround of aircraft. Bhatia was in his games rig, playing a sweaty game of squash that evening, when he suddenly dropped the ball, startled by screaming sirens at the airbase. 'The Pakistan Air Force fighters had come in for a strike. They had kept dusk as "Time on Target" and bombed eleven of our airfields, including Amritsar,' he remembers. 'The game ended right there. We were immediately summoned and asked to be prepared for a retaliatory attack the next morning.

The Amritsar airfield had been bombed and suffered some superficial damage. It was being repaired.' The repairs were completed by 2300 hours, and the next morning the pilots left at dawn and landed in Amritsar, from where they were sent on the first two strikes on 4 December and a third one on 5 December.

Damayanti remembers the evening well. 'When Vijay heard he had to go, he wanted to park his beloved car in a safer place,' she recounts. 'Night was falling, and being wartime, no one was allowed to switch on the lights, so we drove in the dark and parked the car in the cantonment garage. The next morning he left.' That was the last time she saw him.

~

Air Marshal Bhatia feels that Tambay could not have survived the crash because if he had ejected from the plane, Bhatia would have seen it. But he does add a caveat, saying, 'Miracles do happen. I saw his aircraft on fire and called him on the RT set asking him to eject but he did not respond. There is a possibility that he had been incapacitated by the strike and could not respond or he was too busy struggling with his controls. I saw his aircraft crash, but I do wish some miracle happened and he is still alive.'

Damayanti strongly believes that Tambay survived. Her belief comes from many subsequent revelations that point in that direction.

A few days after Vijay went missing, his father came across a Pakistani newspaper which had a report from Dhaka giving out the names of five Indian pilots who had been captured alive. One of the pilots was identified as 'Tombay'. Before going for the war, Tambay and Damayanti had visited the Convent of Jesus and Mary in Ambala, and Vijay had got himself a cross on a chain. He had said that if he was captured he would pretend he was a Christian and give his name as 'Tombay' since the Pakistanis were expected to be more antagonistic towards Hindus.

In a *Time* magazine article dated 27 December 1971, a picture was published of two POWs looking through the bars of a prison cell in Pakistan. While the one standing in front is believed to be Major A.K. Ghosh—also among those missing in action from 1971—Damayanti feels that the man standing behind him (whose face is only partially visible) is Tambay.

In 1979, BBC journalist Victoria Schofield's controversial book *Bhutto: Trial and Execution* was published, in which former Pakistan prime minister Zulfikar Ali Bhutto recounts his experience of not being able to sleep at night because he would hear 'horrific screams in the dead of the night' coming from the cell next to his in the Kot Lakhpat prison. When he tried to find out who those people were, he was told that they were Indian POWs captured in the 1965 and 1971 wars, who had lost their minds. Who were those prisoners who were never repatriated? This is a very valid query.

After the 1971 war ended, approximately 93,000 Pakistani soldiers surrendered, and India took them as

POWs. Pakistan also held a much smaller number. After the Simla Agreement in July 1972, the two countries agreed to exchange POWs and brought out two lists of their prisoners. Tambay's name did not figure in either of them. A third list was awaited but it never came.

~

In November 1972, soon after she received the Arjuna Award, Damayanti took up a job as sports officer in Jawaharlal Nehru University and shifted to Delhi. In 1975, Flt Lt Tambay's cousin, who was an army doctor posted in Jamnagar, called her up. He wanted Damayanti to send him a good photograph of Vijay. He said he had met a Bangladeshi officer in the mess who thought he had met a person called Tambay who was a POW in Lyallpur prison in Pakistan. A hopeful Damayanti took the largest photograph she could find and decided to go to Jamnagar personally.

There, she met T.A. Yusuf, a Bangladeshi naval officer, who recounted a fascinating story. He said that in 1972, officers supporting the new Bangladeshi regime were thrown into prison in Pakistan. Yusuf was one of them. He was imprisoned in Lyallpur Jail (in 1977, the name was changed to Central Jail, Faisalabad), where he met someone who could have been her husband. Yusuf said that one day he crossed over to the cell next to his and discovered a man who was writing something on a wall. Startled by Yusuf's sudden appearance, the prisoner dropped the piece of chalk from his hand. Yusuf noticed that the prisoner had written the name 'Tambay' on the wall. Despite the POW's unkempt beard, Yusuf noticed a scar on his chin. He told Damayanti he particularly noticed that because he himself had a scar on the chin where hair did not grow. He said the POW was of his height (around 5'7") and had curly hair. All three details matched with Tambay. Yusuf said the POW told him that he was a fighter pilot whose plane had crashed in Sargodha. That was the only detail that did not match since Tambay's plane had crashed in Shorkot Road. The two places were close to each other, but Sargodha was better known, so maybe the POW had said 'Sargodha' as a location identifier, Yusuf felt.

'I stayed in Jamnagar for two days,' says Damayanti. 'I spent eight or nine hours with him. I showed him Vijay's photograph. He said he couldn't be sure since the man he saw had a beard. I used a pencil to sketch a beard on Vijay's photograph and implored him to remember something. Anything.' Damayanti is convinced that Yusuf had met Tambay, but Yusuf told her very clearly that whatever he had told her was for her ears only. He would not recount any of it to the Indian government. 'He said, "I don't want to get into any kind of trouble with Pakistan, and if I am asked about this incident officially, I shall deny the story."' Damayanti did write to the government, specifically telling them not to question Yusuf but to find out discreetly from other sources if Tambay was in Lyallpur. 'But they did exactly what I had asked them not to do. They questioned Yusuf and he denied the story. And that was the end of the matter,' she says.

~

In 1989, nearly eighteen years after Vijay had gone missing, his uncle Jayant Jatar was sent to Pakistan as manager of the under-19 cricket team. Jatar met Gen. Tikka Khan at a social event and requested him to let him (Jatar) see Vijay just once. Though the general did not respond then, the next day Jatar was told he would be taken to see his nephew, but he was not to try and talk to him. Jatar was blindfolded and driven for about forty-five minutes, after which he heard the creaking sound of heavy metal gates opening. The car moved ahead and he heard another gate opening. Finally, he was asked to come out of the car and his blindfold was removed. He was shown a prisoner in a cell, 10 feet away, who was reading a newspaper. Jatar recognized him as Vijay. He looked up but did not seem to recognize Jatar, who had deliberately worn his India blazer that day. Jatar tried to point towards the insignia on his blazer to show Vijay that he was from India but did not get any response. When the people who had taken him there noticed what Jatar was doing, they pushed him outside. When he came back to India he met Damayanti and told her about his experience.

~

In 1983 and 2007, two trips were organized where the relatives of missing Indian soldiers were taken to Pakistan and asked to search for their people. Both times they went with a lot of hope but returned disheartened. Damayanti says that in 1983, P.V. Narasimha Rao, who was the external affairs minister, met relatives of six POWs who were going to Pakistan and briefed them personally in Hyderabad House, Delhi. 'He told us that this was the first time that consular access was being given and both countries had agreed to exhibit their POWs to visiting relatives. "You take back yours while we will take back ours" was the agreement.'

Rao explained to them that both countries needed a face-saving approach. In this case, it would be through names. Damayanti says, '"You will need to agree that your people are there under assumed names," he told us. "So if you find your loved one, you will say, *Ye Vijay Tambay hain par inhone apna naam Mohammad Yusuf bataya tha*, which is why he could not be identified earlier." He told us this drama would have to be played out and we agreed. Everything was agreeable to us as long as we got our people back.' The deal was that Pakistan would repatriate forty-five people and India would repatriate thirty.

'We went with so much hope, but the day we reached Lahore, the papers carried the news that India had gone back on its word. Instead of thirty, only three prisoners were shown to the visiting group from Pakistan,' says Damayanti. 'We knew right then that our visit was going to be futile now. They would surely retaliate and not show us our people.' The next day, when the Indians were taken to Multan Jail, as soon as the jailer saw her, he said, 'Mrs Tambay, I am sorry, Tambay is not here.' Later, the prisoners they met told them that their people had been hidden and would not be produced. The team returned to India disappointed. They could not find even one of their soldiers.

In June 2007, fourteen next of kin of the missing people were again sent to Pakistan. This time they were on a fifteen-day tour that received worldwide media attention. This was the first time that the two countries that had been at war were making a humanitarian gesture, and both governments publicized it in a big way. The then defence minister, A.K. Antony, told the visiting team, 'We will pursue this till we find the truth. Don't call them POWs, call them missing in action.' The fourteen boarded an Indian Airlines flight to Lahore on 1 June with a lot of expectations, even though it had been thirty-five years since the war. They visited multiple jails all over Pakistan but had to return disappointed. At each jail, they were only allowed to interact with the jailer and accept his statement on whether any Indian prisoners were being held there or not. They were not allowed to visit jail hospitals, where prisoners who had lost their minds were kept, or even check military detainees. At no point were they allowed to see prisoners face to face. 'It was a useless exercise,' says Damayanti. 'It was quite evident that the governments were making an effort to end our search without any genuine intention to help.'

~

Despite all these disappointments, Damayanti has not given up. She says she always believed he would come back. 'The thought of marrying again never ever crossed my mind.' Now, she says, she has reconciled to the idea that he may never return. 'But I still want to know what happened to him. For our own official machinery he is just another file number. They are ready to go along with whatever Pakistan tells us. They are not personally involved like I am. For me, he was everything and vice versa. If I don't look out for him, who will?'

~

It is time to leave. I want a picture with her but since she lives alone, there is no one to take it for us. I tell her I'll take a selfie. '*Aata hai tumhe? Humein toh nahi aati ye naye zamane ki baatein*,' she says. I turn my cellphone camera on selfie mode and set it up on the dining table. Guiding her to her favourite chair, I set the timer and come back to stand behind her. She is sitting still as a statue, looking at the numbers flashing on the screen. Four. Three. Two. One. 'Smile,' I whisper in her ear. The shutter clicks. 'Did you smile?' I ask. 'I did,' she replies, her eyes sparkling like an incredulous child's. I put my arms around her and give her a hug. And then, with a piece of barfi that she insists I must eat, I sprint downstairs to meet the driver of my cab.

As I drive back home, my thoughts stay with the young fighter pilot who had walked across to his Su-7 with a swagger at Amritsar airbase fifty years ago. I wonder if he still lives in some jail in Pakistan, wrinkled and withered, his spirit broken by torture, loneliness and time. Does he stare with vacant eyes from behind the iron bars of a dark cell? Does he move in chains, his ears now accustomed to the clanging of metal at every step? Does he spend his days sitting alone and forgotten, with cavities in his teeth and hair that has long turned grey and matted? Or has he lost his mind and is screaming expletives at passers-by, not knowing any more where that anger comes from?

My heart sinks at the thought of how many brave soldiers are cruelly shackled away in foreign lands with fading memories of loved ones they will never see again. 'When I visited the prisons, I saw how prisoners were treated. I saw old men with chained ankles being taken to see their relatives from across a barrier,' Mrs Tambay told me. '*Tab ye laga*, I hope he was never alive to suffer this. *Aise jeevan ka kya fayda.*' Her sad eyes shall haunt me for a long time. We say we won the 1971 war. But does that victory mean anything at all when we could not stand up for the soldiers who went to fight for us?

Author's Note

This story is based on interviews with Damayanti Tambay and Air Marshal V.K. Bhatia (retd), PVSM, AVSM, VrC and Bar, who led the mission to bomb Shorkot Road.

Flt Lt V.V. Tambay went missing on 5 December 1971 after his plane crashed inside Pakistan. While initially Pakistan Radio and newspapers reported that he was captured alive, the Pakistan government later claimed that he had died in the crash.

The Government of India believes that eighty-three Indian soldiers are in Pakistan's prisons, and most of that number comes from the two wars of 1965 and 1971. The Government of Pakistan also claims that a smaller number of its soldiers are in Indian prisons. Both nations deny the number of missing in action in their custody, but this incarceration is completely against the Third Geneva Convention of 1949.

Jangi Qaidi

5 December 1971
Uttarlai Airbase (5 km from Barmer)
India
0840 hours

Two daredevil fighter pilots belonging to 220 Squadron, Desert Tigers, are on a ground attack mission. Sqn Ldr K.K. Bakshi, nicknamed Joe, and Flt Lt Jawahar Lal Bhargava, nicknamed Brother, have taken off in their HF-24 aircraft (popularly called the Marut). They have been tasked with crossing the international border and following a route that shall take them to the Pakistani airfield of Naya Chor, from where they have to turn left and go to Umarkot, then turn east and head back to India. Their mission is to identify and destroy targets of opportunity en route—like military trains, tanks, army units, camel convoys and vehicles. The Maruts are fully laden with rockets, guns and bombs.

Nearly fifty years later, Air Commodore J.L. Bhargava leans back on the sofa in his Panchkula bungalow, a boyish smile playing on his lips, and tells me about that day. 'Sometimes, fighter pilots are told to take down pinpointed objectives, but that day we had been told to identify possible targets and destroy them,' he says.

So the two pilots fly low and check out the area carefully.

'We found nothing in Naya Chor,' remembers Bhargava, 'but around the airfield, we spotted Pakistan's field formation units. We swooped down, deployed our rockets and then pulled up quickly. Pilots are trained to get out of the area they have attacked immediately to avoid ricochet fire.'

The first attack goes well, but just as Bhargava is going down for the second, enemy anti-aircraft guns start blazing, and his Marut is caught in a hail of bullets.

~

Naya Chor, Pakistan
0920 hours

Bhargava is about to swoop down for the second attack when he hears the repeated beep of the audio-warning signal. The red light is flashing, and he realizes that his plane is on fire.

The constant beeps of the fire warning in the claustrophobic cockpit are starting to unnerve him. He leans forward to switch it off. A bead of sweat trickles down his forehead. It drips down his face and, making its way past the chinstrap of his helmet, finds its way into his neck.

Bhargava is itching to wipe it off, but his hands are on the control stick that doesn't seem to be responding at all.

The Marut's hydraulics have failed, making it very heavy to the touch, and Bhargava is still struggling with the controls when he finds that his left engine has packed up and his radio communication is disabled. In the vast, unending expanse of the sky, he is now completely alone—and in enemy territory.

He aborts the second attack and turns to head back home. Down below him is an unending stretch of uninhabited desert sand. He releases his bombs to lighten the aircraft load so that it is easier to handle. Altitude is dropping steadily, and as Bhargava crosses a deserted mosque, he realizes that his aircraft speed has fallen drastically.

Staying calm by reminding himself that India is not too far, Bhargava is struggling with the controls when he finds his second engine spluttering. He now knows a crash is inevitable. If he doesn't eject, he will go down with the Marut.

~

Mumbling a prayer, the young pilot pulls the standby ejection handle between his legs that will activate his ejection seat. He doesn't reach for the main ejection handle above his head because for that he will need both hands and at that moment he cannot afford to let go of the control stick.

The standby handle doesn't work. The faces of his young wife, Anu, and Sandeep and Suniti, his children aged three and one, flash before Bhargava's eyes. A cold, numbing fear grips his heart, but he reminds himself that the Marut is known for its zero–zero ejection (at zero height and zero speed). He can make out that he is less than 100 feet above the ground and he should not let go of the joystick because a safe ejection requires that the plane be steady and not in descent. But now he has no choice. As the ground comes rushing up to meet him, Bhargava lets go of the controls and quickly pulls the main ejection handle down with all his strength.

The canopy above him jettisons and, within a fraction of a second, the ejection seat fires. It shudders violently, and Bhargava is flung into the air. The unpiloted aircraft goes out of control and dives down just as the seat separates from Bhargava. He is heading towards the ground with what would have been killing force, but fortunately his parachute opens, breaking the fall. Bhargava finds himself lying on the dunes with the sun scorching his face. He has landed in enemy territory just a little distance away from his crashed Marut that lies with its nose embedded in the sand.

~

Bhargava's fall is broken by his parachute which unfurls in the air just as he touches the ground.

'That, and the fact that I landed in soft sand, saved my life,' he says.

Expecting his plane to explode at any moment, he hastily buries his parachute in the sand, picks up the pilot survival kit (that contains a sleeping bag, a stove, chocolates, four bottles of drinking water, a knife and a compass) and walks away. He can see his comrade Joe circling in the sky. Clambering up a sand dune, Bhargava waves his arms desperately, hoping to catch his attention, but Joe does not spot him. A dejected Bhargava slips out of his olive-green G-suit and hides it in the bushes. Under it, he is wearing yellow trousers and a green fur-collared jersey that he had got from a Sabre flying visit to the US.

Taking the kit to a safe place, he rummages for a map but cannot find one. A plan is starting to form in the feisty fighter pilot's head. He decides that he shall walk east as per his compass and try to cross the border back into India. If caught, he will pretend to be a Pakistani pilot. He sets his watch to Pakistan time, which is half an hour behind Indian Standard Time, and checks his wallet for the Pakistani currency that has been given to each pilot flying across the border. He has Rs 300.

Bhargava is lying low and not leaving the safety of the dunes, when around 1200 hours, he hears snatches of conversation. There are people heading in his direction. Aborting his plan to stay in the desert till nightfall, he removes the extra weight from the survival kit—hiding items like the stove in the bushes—and starts walking east.

~

Dodging a few desert snakes that cross his path, the pilot walks about 3 km, till he spots a village. He has finished all his drinking water and his throat is parched. Hoping to find water, he walks across to a deserted hut. A bearded old man in a dhoti and turban is standing outside. Bhargava lifts his hand in an *adaab*. '*Walekum*,' the man replies. Not having any idea how the greeting is returned, Bhargava takes a deep breath and—with a fleeting remembrance of the times he has spent playing with the nawab of Pataudi when they were both kids (Bhargava's father was employed as the nizam of Pataudi) and even later (when he and Tiger played a Ranji Trophy match for opposing teams)—confidently declares, 'I am Flt Lt Mansoor Ali Khan of the Pakistan Air Force [PAF]. *Mera jahaz crash ho gaya hai. Mujhe peene ka paani chahiye*.' The old man is not impressed. '*Pani nahin hai*,' he replies curtly.

Bhargava notices a cemented pond of stagnated water. 'That is drinking water for camels,' the man says, having followed his gaze. 'If you want, you can drink it.'

Filling up the bottles he is carrying with the murky water, Bhargava gulps it down hastily, hoping his stomach will not act up. Handing over Rs 20 in Pakistani currency to the stranger with the instruction that he should not tell anyone that Mansoor Ali was here, Bhargava prepares to leave. He asks the old man about the village's location and is shocked to find that he is not in Bhitala as he had assumed, but much more to the south, in a place called Pirani Ki Paar. He sets off, changes direction, skirts the sand dunes and walks till he again spots some people and decides to hide. Finding a ditch that is large enough for him to stretch his legs, Bhargava lies down and decides he will now move out only after sunset.

He has barely shut his eyes when he feels eyes on him. Three villagers and a child are looking down at him with curiosity. They want to know who he is. 'I am Flt Lt Mansoor Ali of the PAF. My aircraft was shot down by the Indian Army near Bhitala,' he tells them.

They insist that he accompany them to their village.

'*Mera helicopter aane hi wala hai, wo mujhe Karachi le jayega. Aap chalo*,' Bhargava tells them, hoping they will leave him alone, but they insist that he come with them.

'You are walking towards India. *Aap humare saath chalo*,' they insist.

'How far am I from the border?' Bhargava asks.

'About 12 km,' they answer.

Bhargava has no choice but to accompany them. He plans to escape as soon as he gets the chance.

In the village, he is offered a stringed jute charpoy to sit on while the villagers squat at his feet. The local school's headmaster also joins the gathering and asks Bhargava which part of Pakistan he is from.

'Rawalpindi,' Bhargava replies confidently.

'*Rawalpindi mein kahan rehte hain?*' the headmaster probes further.

Bhargava has no idea about Rawalpindi but makes a wild guess. 'Mall Road,' he replies. His reply seems to convince the suspicious man.

'It was sheer luck that Rawalpindi did have a Mall Road, and later I was kept in a jail there which happened to be just 10 feet from Mall Road,' Air Commodore Bhargava tells me.

As dusk falls, the villagers tell Bhargava that they have informed the Rangers, who will reach the village in a few hours. They offer to make him some tea. Tired and in extreme discomfort since his back has started to hurt, Bhargava is not able to refuse. The time is 1940 hours, and he decides that he will attempt an escape after having the tea. He keeps the knife and four bottles of water in his bag and gives away the rest of his belongings to the village children.

Just as he is gearing up to slip away on the pretext of wanting to relieve himself, four men walk up to him. They are dressed in dark grey Pathani suits and carrying automatic rifles. The Rangers have arrived earlier than expected. Naik Awaz Ali is in charge, with three other soldiers reporting to him. Once again, Bhargava claims that he is Flt Lt Mansoor Ali. He tells Awaz Ali that he needs to answer the call of nature. Awaz Ali sends him out with two armed Rangers.

'I did think about making a dash for freedom, but the moon was in the sky, making the area quite visible, and they both had automatic rifles. I knew they would not hesitate to shoot me down if I tried to run, so I reluctantly returned to the hut,' Bhargava recounts.

He finds Awaz Ali inspecting the gifts he (Bhargava) had handed out to the children. When he finds his watch showing Pakistani time, Awaz Ali looks perplexed. He is trying to make up his mind whether to believe Bhargava or not. '*Humein aap pe shak hai ki aap Hindustani hain*,' he finally says.

Bhargava appears to look affronted. 'If you don't believe me, *apne kisi afsar ko bulao*,' he responds curtly. 'I shall speak to him.'

'*Main bhi afsar hun*,' Awaz Ali replies, to which Bhargava retorts, '*Tum afsar nahi ho, Awaz Ali. Tum naik ho.*' A puzzled Awaz Ali makes a final attempt to discover the truth. '*Theek hai! Agar aap Musalman hain toh kalima suna dijiye*,' he tells Bhargava.

'I was totally foxed,' Bhargava recounts. 'I had no idea what the kalima was. *Maine toh sirf kalam* [pen] *suni thi*.'

Making one more attempt to bluff his way through, Bhargava pleads with the Ranger. 'It has been a long time, Awaz Ali, I have forgotten it. Besides, I have a terrible pain in my back,' he says.

Awaz Ali offers to recite the kalima first. '*Aap mere peeche dohraiye*,' he says.

Bhargava refuses. 'I thought if I recite it wrong, the villagers would beat me up,' he says.

Awaz Ali is now convinced that Bhargava is fooling him. Tapping the butt of his rifle on the floor, he says, '*Bata do aap kaun ho nahin toh humein aur bhi tarike aate hain sach nikalwane ke*.'

Bhargava realizes his game is up. 'I am Flt Lt Jawahar Lal Bhargava, a pilot of the Indian Air Force [IAF],' he says. 'You can kill me if you wish.' With that he resigns himself to fate.

The villagers seem to have taken a liking to Bhargava. They insist on feeding the Indian pilot a hot and spicy chicken curry with rice before he is taken away, and tell the Rangers that he is Pakistan's guest and no harm should come to him. Around 2300 hours, the Rangers mount their camels. Bhargava is blindfolded and handcuffed and placed on the middle camel being ridden by Ranger Mohabbat Ali. As the camel makes its way through the sand dunes in the moonlit night, Bhargava rues his fate. He has been caught just 15 km from the border.

~

The next day, around 1200 hours, Bhargava is alarmed to hear the sound of fighters. He tells the Rangers that they must make their camels sit still, otherwise the IAF planes will bomb them. The Rangers agree and the planes pass, much to Bhargava's relief. Soon after that, some more Rangers join the group. One of them asks Bhargava why he isn't in unform. Bhargava tells him that the G-suit was heavy and he had to take it off. Suspecting him to be a spy, the Ranger tells Awaz Ali, '*Goli maar dalle nu*.' Bhargava pleads with the men to remove his blindfold if they plan to shoot him, but Awaz Ali assures him that he will not be harmed.

As night falls, Bhargava can make out from the conversation that the 'camelcade' is headed towards a village called Chachro. However, when they take a break for water on the way, the Rangers discover that Chachro has been taken over by the Indian Army (in a daring operation by 10 Para) and change their destination. 'Had we reached Chachro that night, I might have been free and the Rangers POWs,' Bhargava smiles wistfully.

~

After five days of painful travelling, Bhargava is brought to the PAF base at Drigh Road, Karachi. He has fond memories of meeting Captain Murtaza of the Pakistan Army on the way, who has Bhargava's blindfold and handcuffs removed and offers him cigarettes and tea. He also offers Bhargava his own shaving kit so Bhargava can groom himself. 'Captain Murtaza looked after me very well, and I was totally impressed by his hospitality. Not once did he give me a hint that I was his enemy and a prisoner,' Bhargava remembers gratefully.

~

Eventually, on 12 December, Bhargava and two other captured IAF pilots—Sqn Ldr A.V. Kamat and Flying Officer Mulla Feroze—are flown to a POW camp in Rawalpindi, where they are placed in solitary confinement and subjected to regular interrogation.

On 25 December, Christmas Day, Bhargava gets a pleasant surprise. He is taken to an interrogation room where he finds many other IAF pilots who are also POWs. 'I met Wg Cdr [later Air Vice Marshal] B.A. Coelho, Sqn Ldr (later Gp Capt.) D.S. Jafa, Sqn Ldr (later Wg Cdr) A.V. Kamat, Flt Lt (later Gp Capt.) Dilip Parulkar, Flt Lt (later Group Capt.) Tejwant Singh, Flt Lt (later AVM) A.V. Pethia, Flt Lt (later Wg Cdr) M.S. Grewal, Flt Lt (later Gp Capt.) Harish Sinhji, Fg Off. (later Wg Cdr) V.S. Chati, Fg Off. (later Air Cmde) K.C. Kuruvilla and Fg Off. (later Wg Cdr) H.N.D. Mulla Feroze. We were a total of twelve people,' recounts Bhargava.

It is an emotional reunion. The camp commandant arranges a Christmas cake for the POWs, and Coelho, being the senior-most, cuts it. Tejwant, who is the last person to have ejected, tells the other POWs about the surrender ceremony which he saw on TV in Amritsar, making smiles light up their gaunt faces. 'It was his bad luck that he became a POW the very next day,' Bhargava relates. The pilots are thrilled to know that they have won the war and Bangladesh has come into being. Their sacrifice has not been in vain.

~

On 12 August 1972, Parulkar, Grewal and Harry escape from the prison. They walk in the rain and boldly get on a bus headed for Peshawar. They manage to reach Landi Kotal village on the Afghan border but are caught while trying to organize a taxi to the border.

The three are brought back and tried in the Rawalpindi camp as per the Geneva Conventions, while the others are blindfolded and handcuffed and driven six hours to Lyallpur jail, where 600 soldiers and seven officers of the Indian Army are already being kept. The three runaways are given a fair trial and punished with twenty-eight days of solitary confinement. In September, they join their comrades at Lyallpur.

'Unlike Rawalpindi, which was a makeshift arrangement, this was a proper jail with cement beds, a thin mattress and a blanket. Every cell had an Indian-style toilet,' Bhargava remembers.

~

In the last week of November, there is a lot of excitement in Lyallpur. The Indian POWs are told that an important dignitary is visiting and they all have to attend his public address. Bhargava, whose back has gradually got worse, is the only one among the Indian POWs who is bedridden. The jail authorities offer to take him on a stretcher but he declines. 'I was in really bad shape; I could barely walk,' he remembers. 'Besides being in immense physical pain, I was psychologically very demoralized too. I was not sure if my back would ever heal.'

He hears snatches of the dignitary's speech floating in through the window of his cell and finds the voice familiar. 'It was President Zulfikar Ali Bhutto,' he says. 'I was surprised that he was in Lyallpur.' After the speech, Bhargava hears a helicopter taking off and the footsteps of the prisoners returning to their cells. One of the POWs, Bahadur, peers in, looking excited. '*Shaab shaab, hum wapish ja rahe hain*,' he says. '*Kahan ja rahe hain?*' a curious Bhargava asks. 'Hindushtan,' replies Bahadur with a big grin on his face. '*Bhutto aaya tha. Ushne kaha tum watan jao, tumhe humnein azaad kar diya*.'

A wave of happiness sweeps over the prison cells as the pilots are filled with hope. They talk and laugh a lot more, looking forward to being with their families once again. Most get haircuts from the army barbers who are also POWs.

~

30 November 1972
Lyallpur jail

All 617 POWs are asked to dress up in the khaki Pakistan Army uniforms provided to them. They are then taken to Lahore by train. On 1 December, buses carry them to the Wagah border. The journey is memorable since the POWs are laughing and talking, and they cross similar buses coming from the Indian border that are bringing the Pakistani *jangi qaidi* who have been released by the Indian government. There is an air of hope and happiness in the air. Brave soldiers of both countries are returning home.

The Indian POWs are kept in tents erected 100 metres from the border. They can hear the band playing on the Indian side. The soldiers wait impatiently for their release orders. Finally, the legal papers arrive and the repatriation process begins. It is done in a sequence, one man at a time. The soldiers go first, followed by the army officers, and finally, it is the turn of the pilots.

There is a moment of heartbreak when the flaps of the tent open and a Pakistani officer steps in. He tells the stunned pilots that they shall not be repatriated and would be sent back to Lyallpur jail. '*Udhar band baj raha hai, dance chal raha hai, aur humko bataya gaya, "Tum wapis nahin jaoge,"*' Bhargava remembers. 'We were shattered.'

To make matters worse, the pilots had taken some parting shots at members of the jail staff who had not been cooperative. '*Hum unko bol ke aaye the ki ab tumhe dekh lenge,* and they had also warned us, "*Hum tumhe dekh lenge*,"' Bhargava says. 'The thought of going back to them was very unnerving.'

The disheartened IAF pilots wait as they are told that efforts are being made to contact Bhutto directly. The confusion has arisen because India has released only the POWS of the western front and none of the pilots. Since Pakistan's pilots have not come back, it has been decided that even the Indian pilots shall not be released. Bhutto declares that he has released all POWs without any conditions and they should be sent back, and the pilots get permission to leave. (The PAF pilots were flown in the next day accompanied by the Indian Army chief, Gen. Sam Manekshaw, himself.)

Finally, at 1130 hours, the pilots cross the border to the sound of a lively band playing and elated people doing the bhangra. Giani Zail Singh, then chief minister of Punjab, stands by to receive them and welcomes each soldier with a warm hug. The Indian Army's elegant black Ambassador cars bring the pilots to the IAF unit in Amritsar, where they are served chilled beer and a hot lunch. 'We had beer after a year,' Bhargava smiles at the memory. Around 1700 hours, there is a civic reception at Company Bagh, Amritsar, after which the ten pilots are flown to Palam in an Avro. They reach Delhi at 2200 hours and are received at the airport by the chief of air staff and their families and friends. Bhargava breaks down when his four-year-old son calls him 'uncle', having forgotten what his father looks like.

~

As we reach the end of the interview, Bhargava offers to recite something for me. '*Laaa Ilaaha Illa-llaahu Muhammadur-Rasoolu-llaah*,' he says. (There is no God but Allah, and Muhammad is the messenger of Allah.) It is the kalima that he did not know in 1971.

'*Seekh liya aapne*?' I ask him with a smile.

'Yes,' he laughs. I switch off my recorder and cap my pen, closing the notebook where I have been jotting down points. 'If I had known the kalima then, my story might have changed,' Air Cmde Bhargava says wistfully.

'That would have made an interesting story too, Flt Lt Mansoor Ali,' I tell him with a smile. The room rings out with his deep-throated, hearty laughter. I marvel at these heroes who not only put their lives at stake for their country but did it with so much spirit and panache.

Author's Note

This story is based on an interview with Air Cmde J.L. Bhargava, who was a POW in Pakistan for a year after his Marut crashed behind enemy lines. He now lives in Panchkula with his wife, Anu. His son went on to become a test pilot in the IAF and his daughter is married to an army officer.

Bhargava was among twelve IAF pilots, seven army officers and 600 soldiers who were made

POWs in Pakistan during the 1971 war. They were the only declared POWs.

Ten pilots were officially released on 1 December 1972, while two pilots—Fg Off. Mulla Feroze and Flt Lt A.V. Pethia—who were sick and injured, were released earlier in February and March 1972 respectively.

Charge of the Gorkhas

On the night of 20 November 1971, which happened to be Eid-ul-Zuha, the soldiers of the 4th Battalion of the 5th Gorkha Rifles (Frontier Force) crossed the international border and entered the heavily defended town of Atgram in East Pakistan with naked *khukri*s in their hands. What followed was a chilling saga of courage and sacrifice that can never be forgotten. It was the Indian Army's first organized attack in 1971.

~

21 November 1971
Around 0330 hours
Atgram, East Pakistan

Rifleman Dil Bahadur Chhetri stands absolutely still. The whites of his eyes glint like fireflies in the dark, but other than that he merges completely with the night, his uniform, helmet and boots dissolving into the shadows. He switches on the flashlight in his hand and moves forward, keeping its beam low. The circle of light falls on a figure lying face down on the ground. Chhetri bends down and turns the body over. It is his platoon commander, Capt. Praveen K. Johri, a bloodied khukri still clasped in his hand. He has been shot. His vacant eyes stare into the sky where a crescent moon hangs in the purple darkness.

A paralysing fear grips Chhetri, who is only twenty-one. It feels like a living, throbbing creature is seeping into every pore of his body and slowly starting to suffocate him. Chhetri can hardly breathe. He remembers his beautiful village in Nepal. An image of his elderly parents flashes before him. His father in his Nepali topi, sitting in the courtyard, smiling at him with eyes that get crow's feet as deep as ravines; his mother in her colourful headscarf and green *pothe ki mala*, looking at him with so much love that it hurts. Chhetri's eyes burn with tears. He wonders if he will ever see them again.

The enemy bunker is right before him. He tries to load his rifle, only to find that it has jammed. Flinging it away, he whips out the khukri hanging at his waist. With a menacing snarl, he pushes open the door of the bunker. Torch in left hand, khukri in right, Chhetri steps inside. Three enemy soldiers are bent over medium machine guns (MMGs), spewing death at his comrades. '*Jai Mahakali*!' he calls out, his voice raised to a high pitch. The soldiers look back in surprise. '*Aayo Gorkhali*!' Skin erupting in goosebumps, eyes breathing fire, Chhetri falls upon them. Screams of terror ring out as the blade cuts into human flesh.

~

January 2021
Kotdwar
Pauri Garhwal

On a cold January morning, I take a taxi to the hill cantonment of Lansdowne. The air nips at my bare nose when I roll down the window and makes me zip up my jacket all the way to my chin. Soon, we cross the town of Dugadda, and the Kho River, which had been winding along companionably beside us, decides to turn left and part ways. After an hour's drive through the twisting and turning mountain track, I reach a perfect, picture-postcard, green-roofed house in Lansdowne where resides eighty-one-year-old Col Yashwant Singh Rawat (retd), who lost a leg in the 1971 war. Seated in his sunlight-dappled sitting room with his wooden leg stretched out in front of him, the smartly dressed old-world colonel sips on steaming hot broccoli soup and tells me this story of unbelievable human courage.

~

19 November 1971
Panchgram, Silchar district
India

A tall, handsome man with an intimidating moustache, Lt Col Arun Bhimrao Harolikar, commanding officer (CO) of 4/5 Gorkha Rifles, is addressing the uniformed men sitting in front of him. He has called a meeting of his Order (O) group which comprises young officers, most of them in their twenties. 'The time to cross the border has come, gentlemen,' he says, watching the sparkle that lights up most of the eyes looking up at him. 'Orders have been received. We shall be attacking Atgram tomorrow.' Smiles spread across the faces in front of him. Colonel Harolikar, however, is grim. 'The battle shall be fought with khukris,' he says. 'Tell the boys to sharpen their weapons.'

Second Lieutenant Rajinder Singh Sahrawat, who has joined the battalion just the previous day, is among those listening. He is twenty-one years old and has just returned after completing the young officers' course at Belgaum. The choice of weapon takes him by surprise, as it does many others. 'The fact that he wanted us to use khukris and not rifles came as a bit of a shock,' he tells me in an interview forty-nine years later. 'The Gorkhas had a reputation of using their khukris with lethal effect in close combat, but this time we would be attacking an enemy position that was heavily fortified with medium and light machine guns [MMGs and LMGs],' he says. 'But, of course, no one had the guts to question the CO. We were really young then and thrilled at the thought that we would be slicing the enemy with our khukris.' A smile plays on his face.

Col Harolikar discloses his attack plan. The battalion would move to a gully about a kilometre from the Indian border outpost (BOP) at Natanpur after last light and then stay under cover through the next day. At night, it would cross the Surma River that marked the border between India and East Pakistan, and attack Atgram. He makes two things very clear. Khukris would be the main mode of attack. And the surprise factor would be crucial. To ensure that even enemy BOPs are not alerted that the Indian Army has crossed into East Pakistan, the men are instructed to maintain complete silence and not retaliate even if enemy BOPs fire at them.

Col Harolikar gives instructions to his company commanders. The attack group, comprising Alfa Company under Maj. Dinesh Rana and Delta Company under Maj. Rattan Kaul, will lead; Bravo Company under Capt. Virendra Rawat and Charlie Company under Maj. Maney Malik will lay roadblocks on the two roads exiting Atgram to ensure no enemy soldiers escape and no reinforcements reach the enemy from outside. Charlie is marked as the reserve company for the attack. If that attack happens, then it is to be launched under Maj. Shyam Kelkar, battalion second-in-command (2IC).

While COs usually take a safe position in war for the very logical reason that they need to stay alive to take decisions, Col Harolikar decides against it. 'The CO's group will be positioned right behind the attacking party,' he says. Writing his memoirs many years later, he explains why he took that decision, giving two reasons. The first was that he was new to the unit then (just three months old) and wanted to win the respect of his men by assuring them that even he was ready to risk his life along with them. The second was that he wanted to be up front so that he could assess the situation and give quick commands while the battle was going on.

Artillery battery commander Maj. Krishan Dev Segan of 99 Mountain Regiment and his team are told to accompany the CO so that artillery fire can be brought on to the enemy within seconds, if required. Officers of other supporting arms (engineers and medical corps) are told to stay back and join at Atgram in the morning after the battle is over. 'They were really disappointed,' Maj. Sahrawat remembers. He says that Capt. Amit Sarkar, a young engineer officer with the unit, who also happened to be his immediate senior from the National Defence Academy, was devastated. 'He kept telling me it was very unfair. So, like a good comrade, I told him to ignore the CO's orders and come along quietly since no one would notice him in the chaos of war. His face lit up and eventually he did join us in battle.'

~

After the address is over, unit 2IC Col Kelkar goes across to twenty-five-year-old Capt. Himkar Vallabh Pandey and Capt. Praveen K. Johri, who is a year and a half younger. Captain Pandey, now seventy-five and settled in Pune, remembers the conversation clearly. 'Major Kelkar told us quite frankly that it was going to be a suicidal attack. He said intelligence reports had hinted that the bunkers were heavily fortified, so chances of returning alive were bleak.' Pandey says he and Johri were given a choice. '"One of you has to lead the attack," he told us.'

Both officers immediately volunteer to go. '*Agar suicidal attack hai toh main jaunga*,' insists Pandey, who is from Alfa Company. Johri, who is from Charlie, is outraged. '*Main darta hun kya*?' he asks. 'Why can't I go? *Main jaunga*.' Col Kelkar, who knows the two of them have been good friends since the day they joined the unit on the same date in Jalandhar, leaves the final decision to them.

Capt. Pandey says he and Johri argued about it for a while till Johri clinched it by saying that since Pandey was married and responsible for his wife and six-month-old son, it was the unmarried Johri who should be going. 'He told me, "You are a family man. I have no responsibilities. Let me go."' He also added that since his father (a retired warrant officer from the air force) was alive and he (Johri) had taken an insurance policy of Rs 1.2 lakh in the name of his three younger sisters, the family was financially well taken care of too. 'If something happens to me, each of my sisters shall get Rs 40,000. I have no worries,' he says. Finally, Pandey agrees and a smiling Johri informs the 2IC that he will be leading the attack.

The gentle and soft-spoken Lt Hawa Singh, twenty-one, also in Alfa Company, has been listening quietly all this while. A short-service commission officer, barely two years old in the unit, he comes from a very humble background and is the best basketball player in the battalion. He tells Maj. Kelkar that leading the attack would be an honour for him. 'He was a very brave man,' remembers Capt. Pandey. 'He told the 2IC, "Sir, you have given an option to Capt.

Pandey and Capt. Johri, but please don't even think of considering a substitute for me. I want to do this myself.'" And with that he walks away. Johri and Hawa Singh look at the opportunity to fight for their country with so much *josh* that they both get their heads shaved by the unit barber before leaving Panchgram.

~

The cookhouse gets busy frying shakkarparas, a long-lasting snack made of white flour and sugar, which will be carried by the men as emergency rations. The soldiers start sharpening their khukris. Many of them take out their *chakmak*s (small knives) and start running these along the blades to get that desired .01 mm edge that still reflects light but is capable of slicing smoothly through human skin, muscle and bone if used with the right technique and force. Water bottles are filled up and the men meticulously check their backpacks, boots and helmets for any signs of damage. Regimental medical officer (RMO) Capt. D.K. Sen Gupta asks his team to assemble stocks of painkillers, antibiotics, antiseptics and bandages. He also tells them to add a few bottles of brandy, which will help in dulling pain and enable the injured to deal better with the shock of grievous injury. Sen Gupta watches the soldiers with worried eyes. He knows that many would become battle casualties the next time he sees them.

~

19 November 1971
Last light

The soldiers are served a hot dinner of bhaat, dal and vegetables, but appetites are small. Every man forces himself to eat, though, knowing full well that there are no guarantees on when they will get their next meal.

A stocky Garhwali officer of medium height stands quietly near a tent. Capt. Yashwant Singh Rawat, Bravo Company, is watching his men stuff their pockets with shakkarparas. Many of them are not yet twenty. With their clean-shaven faces, sparkling eyes and crew cuts, they look even younger. His heart fills with affection for them. He knows the shakkarparas will be their only source of energy in battle. After the crowd has cleared, he moves forward to get some for himself.

When dusk falls and shadows start darkening under the trees, the soldiers line up in their assigned sections behind two young Mukti Bahini guides who know the area like the back of their hands. They all start walking. The soldiers have 7.62 mm rifles slung across their shoulders. They have grenades and ammunition in their front packs. From their waists dangle the deadly khukris. The shining blade rests against the muslin lining the scabbard. It hangs from their belts and rests on their hips, instilling confidence each time it rubs against the fabric of their trousers.

Taking off his helmet, Rawat pushes it into his backpack and starts walking alongside his company. He finds that most of the soldiers have also taken theirs off since the heavy steel helmets are uncomfortable to wear. They can afford to do that because the battalion is still on the Indian side of the border and there are no fears of being shot. Rawat's mind is on Uma, his young wife, and their nine-month-old daughter, Tanu. He wonders if she has started crawling yet.

It does not take the soldiers long to reach the pre-marked gully where they settle down for the night. Nearly all lie awake, with their hearts beating faster than ever before. Some eventually doze off, their heads supported by their backpacks. Others lie in the darkness with eyes shut, remembering the loved ones they have left behind. Col Harolikar closes his eyes and tries to sleep. His thoughts go to his wife, Jaya, and daughter, Anjali, who is seven. He doesn't know what the next night will bring for him and his boys, but he feels a suffocating sense of responsibility for them all.

~

20–21 November 1971
Night of the attack

It is Eid. A crescent moon dangles in the sky, a sliver of exquisite beauty. The Gorkhas hardly notice it as they start lacing up their boots. One platoon after another, they slowly emerge from the gully, and like ghosts in the darkness start to follow the two guides who are leading them to the banks of the gently flowing Surma, the river that marks the boundary between India and East Pakistan. It is nearly 45 feet wide, and the water sparkles in the moonlight. They have been told that 108 Engineer Regiment will be there to help them go across, but there is no sign of anyone on the riverbank. The Gorkhas sit on their haunches, waiting silently in the darkness. Around 2030 hours, they hear the soft growl of vehicles, and Col Harolikar breathes a sigh of relief to find army vehicles being driven in their direction with headlights switched off. The engineers have arrived. They offload rubber boats that are quickly inflated using foot pumps and put in the water.

Taking thirty men at a time, the engineers ferry the entire battalion across, making sure all lights are concealed and there is as little noise as possible when their oars splash through the water. Around midnight, the entire battalion is deposited on the other bank. The engineers doff their caps to the soldiers and row back. The Gorkhas make no noise, light no cigarettes. The plan is to attack the enemy bunkers between 0100 hours and 0300 hours, when the sentries are expected to be at their sleepiest and their responses dulled.

~

The battalion has about 10 km to cover. Leading the march is Alfa Company's fearless and ever-smiling Capt. Praveen K. Johri. He is by far the most stylish man in the unit and has been ticked off multiple times by his CO for wearing his hair long. Tonight, his freshly shaved head is bare and reflects the fading light of dusk when he takes his helmet off. Along with him are his radio operator and runners, and two sections of his platoon. Company commander Maj. Dinesh

Rana follows with his men and the CO's party. Behind him march the two remaining platoons commanded by Lt Hawa Singh, who looks almost like a twin to Johri with his head shaved as well, and Subedar Ran Bahadur. Only Hawa Singh and Johri know why they have decided to shave their heads. The secret is never revealed since both are destined never to return from Atgram.

The soldiers march across slushy paddy fields that sparkle in the dark and are cumbersome to cross since the cold water seeps into their boots, making their cotton socks cling to their toes. They also try to be as quiet as possible since any noise can set dogs barking and alert the enemy.

Eventually, their fears come true. The silence of the night is interrupted by small-arm enemy fire. The Gorkhas flop down to the ground. The crescendo of fire increases and is joined by LMG fire and calls of 'Allah hu Akbar'. The Pakistani BOPs probably suspect that Mukti Bahini cadres are out there in the fields and planning to create some trouble. They have no idea that the Indian Army has crossed the border. The Mukti Bahini soldiers are known to come quietly in the night and blow up bridges, lay ambushes and disrupt communication, but the Pakistanis are confident in the belief that gunfire will scare them off. The Indian troops remember their instructions and lie sprawled in the wet fields with their heads down, bullets zipping over their helmets. In about forty-five minutes, the firing reduces and eventually the enemy guns fall silent. Finding no response, the Pakistanis believe they have frightened the intruders away.

However, there is a setback. The two Mukti Bahini guides have disappeared in the chaos, and the battalion now has no idea which direction to take. In his memoirs, the late Col Harolikar remembers, 'It was 1 a.m. [when the fire died down]. I thought we were about 2 km short of our objective. But where was Atgram? In which direction?' Standing in a marsh, he holds a whispered consultation with his officers and gets on the radio set with Brigadier C.A. Quinn, commander, 59 Mountain Brigade (who has been on listening watch, knowing that 4/5 Gorkha Rifles is attacking Atgram that night). He asks Quinn for advice on what to do next. Suddenly, a medium machine gun fires in the distance and a smile plays on Harolikar's lips. He knows that only Atgram has MMGs. 'It was a signal from the enemy saying "Come hither",' he writes in his narrative. The soldiers start walking in the direction of the firing.

~

Meanwhile, Charlie Company, which has been tasked with establishing a roadblock on the Atgram–Zakiganj road, is being led by Maj. Maney Malik. Clueless about which direction to take after the two Mukti Bahini guides disappear, the soldiers find themselves in the middle of a muddy field. They are splashing through knee-deep slush and weeds which their boots get entangled in; some soldiers even lose their boots that have to be fished out of the water. Malik takes a quick decision and changes direction. Turning right, he asks his men to follow. They have moved a short distance when his company suddenly comes under heavy machine gun fire. He realizes the enemy BOPs have detected movement. As instructed earlier, the soldiers make no move to return fire, exhibiting extreme restraint. They flop down to the ground and lie uneasily in the darkness as bullets zip over their heads. After nearly fifteen minutes of firing, they hear someone call out, 'Mohamed Afzal, stop firing. It must be the Mukti Bahini out on routine patrol.' Much to Malik's relief, the firing stops.

Young and enthusiastic Capt. Ravinder Singh, eager for battle, crawls over to his company commander and whispers into Malik's ear, '*Sir, Pakistan ki post hai.* Let's attack and capture it.'

'No!' replies an exasperated Malik. 'We haven't been tasked to do that. It will jeopardize the CO's plan.'

Looking back forty-nine years later, Col Malik says, 'Thank goodness we did not do that. We would have exposed our position. Our battalion would have become a sitting-duck target for the enemy, since the attacking companies had not reached Atgram yet.'

~

Around the same time, Col Harolikar and the attacking companies are standing in front of a seven-foot-tall embankment on top of which they can vaguely make out a road. Climbing up, they stand silently in the dark, observing enemy defences, hearts pounding. They feel the khukris resting against their hips. None of them has used one to kill a man before. They know that is going to change tonight.

~

21 November 1971
Around 0300 hours

Atgram appears like a fortress surrounded by inverted L-shaped cement and concrete bunkers. All of a sudden, a few Pakistani soldiers appear on the road. Surprised at seeing unknown men, they shout, '*Kaun hai! Haath khada karo*.' A blood-curdling cry of '*Jai Mahakali! Aayo Gorkhali!*' rings out in the darkness. Every single Gorkha whips out his khukri and leaps forward. Before the Pakistanis can realize what is happening, the soldiers are upon them. The slaughter has begun.

The sounds of battle are heard and the Pakistanis open MMG and mortar fire on the road. Though lethal, the fire does not deter the Gorkhas, who sprint across and leap to the other side in one wave after another. These are the braves of Alfa and Delta companies (Platoons 1–3 and 10–12 respectively). Those caught in the fire fall but their comrades step across their bodies and move forward, with fire in their eyes and flashing blades in their hands. Ignoring the hail of bullets, they make their way to the enemy bunkers.

~

No. 1 Platoon under Captain Johri goes in for the western defences. No. 2 Platoon under Lt Hawa Singh penetrates through the barracks. And No. 3 Platoon under Subedar Ran Bahadur Gurung takes on the defences right of No. 2 Platoon. Soon, flesh is flying all around. Writhing bodies with heads hacked and bent at queer angles lie everywhere. Col Harolikar and his group charge right behind the assaulting company as they move from bunker to bunker with blood-stained khukris in their hands, slaughtering whoever comes in their way. 'I found myself drawn by an unknown and inexorable force, running forward along with my comrades-in-arms. The charge was like a wave with its own momentum and I could hear and faintly discern our brave jawans with their drawn khukris—now bloodied—moving from bunker to bunker, slaughtering one and all. It was as if all of us were possessed by superhuman powers,' writes Col Harolikar.

He is about to enter an enemy bunker when Subedar Ran Bahadur Gurung steps forward, signalling to him that there are enemy soldiers inside. Unpinning a grenade with his mouth, Ran Bahadur makes his way to the firing slit of the bunker and flings it inside. There is a deafening explosion that kills the two enemy soldiers inside and silences the guns.

Meanwhile, No. 1 Platoon, under Capt. Johri, encounters a roadblock. Johri steps forward with his khukri and clears the bunker but is shot dead. An MMG is firing continuously in their direction from another bunker right ahead and not letting them move further. Rifleman Phas

Bahadur Pun runs left and, getting behind the bunker, sprints towards the closed door with his unsheathed khukri in his hand. Pushing it open, he disappears into the dark chasm. Screams ring out from inside the bunker, and the guns fall silent as a victorious Pun steps out. He is moving towards the next bunker when a burst of enemy automatic fire hits him. Bleeding profusely, Pun drops his khukri. He knows his time is up but, making one final superhuman effort, he reaches out for a grenade. Using the last vestige of his energy, he grips the pin with his teeth, pulls it off and lobs the grenade inside the bunker. There is a blast and thick fumes start spooling out of the destroyed bunker as Pun falls to the ground.

No. 2 Platoon, under young Lt Hawa Singh, has penetrated the Pakistani barracks, destroying bunkers and defences behind the main building and along the road. Leading the charge, Hawa Singh moves swiftly towards the small door at the rear of a bunker and tries to push it open. When it doesn't budge, he moves back a little and comes running to kick it hard. It breaks opens and he rushes inside with the impact. He manages to throw a grenade and kill the occupants of the bunker but is repeatedly shot, with the bullets ripping his stomach open. His men lay him down on a bamboo cot inside the bunker. Meanwhile, Alfa Company commander, Major Rana, has spotted defences towards Chargram Bridge and orders the platoon to clear that area next. The platoon havildar takes charge and the platoon moves on reluctantly, leaving a dying Hawa Singh behind. Subedar Bhobilal Pun, mortar fire controller (MFC) with the company, is shot just as the soldiers reach Chargram Bridge. He too has to be left behind as the platoon moves on to complete the task at hand.

As Col Harolikar's notes mention, he enters a bunker, where he hears the hoarse whisper of someone asking for water. He goes in to find Lt Hawa Singh lying on a cot, with his stomach ripped open. He has taken ten bullets and is in unbearable pain. Col Harolikar rushes to his side and calls out for water to be brought. Hawa Singh manages to sip some from the hands of a comrade but dies within an hour. Later, it is found that one of the bullets had pierced his spleen. A simple Jat from Haryana, he had been the sole support for his younger brothers and sisters back home and had gone for the attack knowing he might not come back.

There are many stories of incredible bravery from that night. Early in the attack by No. 1 Platoon of Alfa Company, Dil Bahadur Chhetri's rifle stops firing. He flings it away and moves ahead with his khukri in his right hand and his torch in the left. He finds a bunker and goes inside to see three enemy soldiers, whom he massacres in cold blood. He comes out with bloodshot eyes and blood dripping from his khukri and enters the next bunker. He repeats the carnage, slaying two enemy soldiers with his khukri. When he emerges from the bunker, he finds that a tall and hefty Pakistani soldier has lifted the small-built Lance Naik Joom Bahadur Gurung by the neck. Gurung is dangling in mid-air with his arms and legs flailing around. A furious Dil Bahadur charges. He jumps in the air and, with a powerful swing of his arm, cuts off the enemy soldier's head. It rolls to the ground while his torso is left standing for a few seconds. The man's fingers unclasp, letting go of a surprised Gurung, who drops to his feet and watches his assailant fall.

Col Harolikar mentions running into Rifleman Dil Bahadur Chhetri engaged in what he calls 'the dance of death'. 'I found Chhetri with his bloodied khukri in his hand, emitting sounds which were a mixture of laughter and the cry of an insane man. And it was a death dance with a number of dead bodies with decapitated heads hanging loosely at different angles lying around him,' he writes.

A Narrow Escape

Harolikar himself has a narrow escape. Entering a large bunker that appears to be the enemy's company headquarters, he finds around ten enemy soldiers lying dead. He is standing close to a tall and well-built soldier laid out on the ground when he hears Maj. Rattan Kaul shout, 'Sir, look out!' Harolikar turns to see that the enemy soldier is alive and moving his hand towards his rifle. He jumps on the enemy soldier just as the latter is about to pick up his rifle, a deadly Chinese-make carbine. The two grapple with each other as Kaul moves close to the entwined figures and tries to fire twice, but both times his rifle misfires. Subedar Ran Bahadur Gurung, who happens to be standing nearby, lifts his own rifle and hits the Pakistani soldier hard on the head with its butt, and then shoots a burst of bullets, killing him on the spot.

The dead Pakistani is identified as Maj. Azhar Alvi, company commander of Bravo Company, 31 Punjab, Pakistan Army. Though Alvi has made a crafty but valiant attempt to kill Harolikar, he has been unsuccessful. Col Harolikar acknowledges Alvi as a brave and courageous soldier who opted for a dignified death in the best tradition of the troops he commanded and for the country he served. A letter is found in Maj. Alvi's bunker. It has been written by the officer's wife from Pakistan. 'We worry so much about you all the time; you must come back soon,' she has written, regretting the futility of war and praying to Allah for his long life. The officers who read it understand the pain of the lady who will never see her husband again.

~

The three Delta Company platoons are also on the move. No. 10 Platoon, under 2nd Lt Yang Bharat, crosses the Atgram–Zakiganj road, turns diagonally right and charges at fortifications in the area, destroying them one by one. No. 11 Platoon, led by Subedar Tirtha Bahadur, gets down to clearing a sentry post on the same road. The platoon is fired upon from an LMG bunker. Leading from the front, Tirtha Bahadur fires a burst of his machine gun to kill the occupants.

At this stage, an MMG fires at the platoon, pinning down one of its sections. The 57 mm RCL detachment, with company commander Major Kaul, immediately targets the bunker and destroys it. The platoon encounters Col

Harolikar, who asks the soldiers to hurry up as it will be dawn soon. The section that had been pinned down now charges at the fortification ahead, led by Rifleman Than Bahadur, who is hit by a bullet straight in the head. Firing from Atgram High Ground is eventually neutralized by No. 12 Platoon.

~

Some acts of bravery go unobserved in the fervour of battle but are recorded after it ends. Col Harolikar's notes describe how he finds Captain Johri lying face down with a blood-stained khukri in his hand. His eyes move to the still body of an enemy soldier lying near him. Later, he is told that Johri bravely entered an enemy bunker and destroyed it along with its two occupants. The ever-smiling Johri, who had volunteered for the attack, has died a hero's death.

~

Meanwhile, the RMO, Capt. D.K. Sen Gupta, has received orders to reach the battlefield. He desperately sprints across the fields with his light-man pack and team in tow. His party come under fire from the enemy BOPs. Sen Gupta's medical assistant is shot and he himself has a narrow escape when a bullet hits his helmet. He carries on undeterred and enters Atgram running within an hour of the capture and immediately gets busy tending to the injured. He is unfortunately too late for Hawa Singh, who is dead by then, and Rifleman Phas Bahadur Pun, whose still body lies next to the smoking bunker that he destroyed.

The battle is waning when the first rays of the sun slowly start turning the night sky orange. As the sound of firing and grenades recedes, it becomes evident that the battle is turning in favour of the Gorkhas. Slowly, the firing dies down. By first light, there is an eerie silence in the battlefield and the braves of 4/5 Gorkha Rifles start collecting together, faces smeared with gunpowder, eyes bloodshot, uniforms ripped and stained with blood. Bodies lie scattered all around. The number of loose shoes lying everywhere speak of how the enemy soldiers have been caught unawares.

Atgram has been captured, but at a heavy price. 4/5 Gorkha Rifles has lost two officers, one junior commissioned officer (JCO) and three other ranks, while twenty-two others are wounded. On the enemy's side, B Company of Pakistan's 31 Punjab unit loses one officer and nearly twenty soldiers. The rest manage to run away.

~

No POWs are taken. The enemy has either been killed or has fled, carrying tales of blood-curdling violence. For the Pakistanis, the sheer horror of a khukri attack, which they have never experienced, had been so paralysing that many of those attacked could not even fire their rifles due to shock. 'The khukris created so much terror that the enemy soldiers who survived ran to the 9 Guards unit nearby and surrendered to them, pleading, "Please save our lives. The Gorkhas are cutting our heads off. Don't let them catch us." This was conveyed to us by the CO of the nearby guards unit later,' remembers Col Yashwant Singh Rawat.

Maj. Sahrawat seconds this. 'Only then did we understand why Col Harolikar had insisted on a khukri attack. It instilled abject fear in the enemy and also cut our casualties in the next battle: our attack on the Sagarnal tea estate. When the Pakistanis heard that the Gorkhas were coming, they fled, leaving their posts unoccupied. If it was not war, it would have counted as a comical scene where we were mounting an assault and they were running away instead of putting up a defence. Their will to fight had been completely broken by the Battle of Atgram. We just went and occupied their posts without any resistance,' he remembers.

~

The battalion reorganizes and immediately begins a search for the wounded and dead. 'It was not easy because bodies were lying in the vegetation and visibility was low. Those who were crying out in pain or able to call out were picked up immediately; the others were found as day broke,' Col Rawat remembers. Sen Gupta sets up a medical inspection room in one of the barracks and starts attending to the wounded. His main challenge is to handle shocked and badly injured soldiers, many of whom are in great pain and bleeding profusely. He hands out large pegs of brandy and implores the wounded to drink up before injecting them with painkillers and sedatives.

The Pakistanis have two Toyota vehicles parked at Atgram which the unit takes charge of. These are used to ferry casualties and evacuate those in serious condition to the nearest military set-up.

~

Around midnight on 21–22 November, young Yashwant Singh Rawat and his boys are on guard duty at Atgram. The distant sound of gunfire that had interrupted the stillness of the night has died down. They notice a group of men in khaki uniforms walking in their direction. The pale moonlight falls on their unfamiliar faces. It is an enemy patrol. '*Goli maaro sahab, Pakistani hain*,' yells the JCO with Rawat. The enemy soldiers also reach for their weapons but the alert JCO and Rawat open LMG fire, shooting down two of the Pakistani soldiers. The others in the patrol disappear in the darkness, leaving their dead comrades behind. No other enemy reinforcements dare to come near Atgram thereafter. Late in the night, the battalion's B echelon, responsible for logistic liaison duties, also arrives carrying rations and water. The cookhouse gets to work and the hungry, dehydrated and battle-weary Gorkhas finally get a fresh hot meal. Not many have an appetite for it, though.

The Battle of Atgram is over. It has been won. Yet, when the moon rises that night, in the vacant eyes of the young soldiers who have survived and are finally taking off their helmets and boots to rest in the cold, wet, mushy trenches, there is only sadness and a sense of immense personal loss. Friends they would talk and joke around with till just a day earlier have given up their lives in battle. Both armies have lost young soldiers who had their entire lives in front of them—they will never return to their families. Brave men in uniform have paid the price for political battles.

~

On the night of 3 December 1971, 4/5 Gorkha Rifles attacked Gazipur, defended by Pakistan's 22 Baluch. The Gorkhas emerged victorious once again but paid a heavy price for their victory. The battalion lost its second-in-command, Major Kelkar, and ten other ranks in the battle. Four officers, two JCOs and fifty-seven other ranks suffered serious injuries. Among these were Col Yashwant Singh Rawat, who lost his leg in a grenade blast, and Maj. Sahrawat, who got two bullets in his leg along with splinters, two of which are still lodged in his body.

On the enemy side, nearly thirty enemy soldiers were killed while forty were injured. Demoralized and shaken, Pakistan's 22 Baluch fled to the north, where it was destined to meet 4/5 Gorkha Rifles once again in the Battle of Sylhet.

Author's Note

This story is based on interviews with Col Yashwant Singh Rawat (retd), Col Man Mohan Malik (retd), Maj. Rajesh Singh Sahrawat (retd), Capt. Hemkar Vallabh Pandey (retd) and Col T.D. Gopalkrishna (retd) of 4/5 Gorkha Rifles. Col Malik and Major Sahrawat also read the final battle account to ensure that it was factually correct. The notes of late Brig. Arun Bhimrao Harolikar, MVC, and Lance Havildar Dil Bahadur Chhetri, MVC, who has become hard of hearing now but painstakingly wrote down his experience in Gorkhali for me (which was translated into Hindi by Col TD) have been used to fill in details.

The bodies of Capt. Johri, Lt Hawa Singh, Subedar Bhobilal Pun, Rifleman Phas Bahadur Pun and the other martyrs were taken back across the border and cremated on the banks of the river, wrapped up in blankets since the wood cut from the forest was not dry enough to burn properly. The families of the deceased were informed of their sacrifice through telegrams and phone calls. Capt. Pandey managed to call Capt. Praveen K. Johri's house through the Brigade Exchange and informed his inconsolable parents about his demise. He took leave a few months later and visited their house in Bareilly. 'Praveen used to talk about you a lot. *Wo bolta tha ki hum itne achhe dost hain ki ek dusre ke liye jaan de sakte hain*,' Johri's mother told Pandey. 'Since Praveen is now gone, I see him in you,' she said, making him break into tears, mourning the loss of a friend who gave up his life for him.

Citations

Col Harolikar and Rifleman Dil Bahadur Chhetri were awarded the Maha Vir Chakra for gallantry.

Lt Hawa Singh and Rifleman Phas Bahadur Pun were posthumously awarded the Vir Chakra for their exceptional bravery.

Capt. D.K. Sen Gupta was also awarded the Sena Medal for his selfless devotion to duty and for attending to the injured with absolutely no concerns for his own safety.

Capt. Praveen K. Johri was posthumously awarded the Sena Medal for his gallantry. Naib Subedar Tirtha Bahadur Gurung was also awarded the Sena Medal.

Maj. Azhar Alvi was awarded the Hilal-e-Jurat, Pakistan's second-highest gallantry award, equivalent to the Maha Vir Chakra.

It Can Happen to Anybody

In December 1971, Capt. (later Col) Yashwant Singh Rawat's leg was blown up in a grenade attack during the Battle of Gazipur. He was being evacuated along with the other battle casualties by a hospital train that would take them to Lucknow Command Hospital, where they would undergo treatment and amputations, if required. The injured soldiers were at Dharmanagar Railway Station, in the same coach, when Rawat, who was lying on a berth—in immense pain, since part of his foot had been completely blown up—saw a familiar figure through the window heading towards him. It was Maj. (later Maj. Gen.) Ian Cardozo, who had just arrived and was going to join the battalion in the war front.

'I saw Maj. Cardozo in the distance. He was in his uniform, walking up and down the platform smartly, holding a rolled-up issue of *Time* magazine in his hand. He had heard that the battalion's injured soldiers were being evacuated and had come to the railway station to meet us,' Col Rawat remembers.

Maj. Cardozo climbed into the coach and said, 'Hello, Yashwant! How are you?'

'I told him I had injured my leg and might lose it,' Col Rawat says.

At that, Cardozo smiled and told him, 'Don't worry. That is just luck. It can happen to anyone. Today it has happened to you, tomorrow it might happen to me.' And, telling Rawat to be strong, he walked away, saying, 'You will be fine.'

Rawat was sent off in the train, where the soldiers were accommodated on berths and had nurses attending to them. Cardozo moved on to join 4/5 Gorkha Rifles as second-in-command. He was helicopter-dropped right in the middle of the Battle of Sylhet, since the unit had lost its second-in-command in the Battle of Gazipur. Meanwhile, the special train carrying the war-wounded left for Lucknow. Rawat's leg was amputated at Lucknow and he was moved to the Pune Military Hospital. Guess who was standing in the corridor on one leg, supported with crutches, waiting to greet him when he reached the Pune Military Hospital? None other than Maj. Cardozo, who had been with his unit in Sylhet but had later stepped on a mine and had his foot blown up at the end of the war. He had been evacuated by helicopter, so he had ended up reaching the Pune Military Hospital earlier than Rawat. 'He had a big smile on his face. "I told you it could happen to anyone," he said. "See, it happened to me,"' Col Rawat remembers fondly.

Col Rawat recalls how he was the only man with an amputated leg in Lucknow Command Hospital. Cardozo had already been sent to Pune. 'After my amputation, when I was shifted to the Artificial Limb Centre, Pune, I found that every second man was on one leg.' All the happy-go-lucky amputees in the centre wore their amputated limbs like war medals and went ahead to form the One-Legged Club. It was very active socially. 'We would ask for a vehicle and go to restaurants, cinemas, markets—just about anywhere—on our crutches and generally have a good time. No one had any regrets about lost legs,' Col Rawat remembers. Maj. Abu Tahir of the Bangladesh Army and Maj. Kipgen of the Assam Regiment were the other two members of the One-Legged Club. One day, all four of them dressed up in formal shirts and trousers and even marched into a studio to get a photograph taken.

Gen. Cardozo and Col Rawat are still very good friends, and whenever Col Rawat, who lives in the hill cantonment of Lansdowne, visits Delhi to meet his children, he makes it a point to go and have a drink with his old friend. The two of them exchange old memories of the war and fondly remember comrades who never came back.

Premonition

On the night of 4 December 1971, 4/5 Gorkha Rifles has to attack Gazipur—their third offensive after Atgram and Sagarnal. Maj. S.G. Kelkar, the battalion second-in-command, goes up to commanding officer Col Harolikar and insists that he wants to participate in the battle. Col Harolikar is reluctant to let him do that, and Kelkar loses his patience. 'Sir, I did not get an opportunity to fight in Atgram. This time also you are not allowing me to go to war. *Aap mujhe wapis hi bhej dijiye. Agar mujhe ladai mein jana nahin hai toh main yahan kya kar raha hun?*' Kelkar tells the CO, getting very upset. Col Harolikar finally agrees, though reluctantly, and makes Kelkar incharge of the third phase of the attack which is to be led by Bravo and Charlie companies.

Since 2000 hours has been fixed as time of movement from the concentration area, soldiers are told to rest for a few hours so that they will be fresh for battle. 'Since there was no food, we munched on the shakkarparas we were carrying in our pockets, and then, with our heads resting on our haversacks, both Maj. Kelkar and I lay down next to each other,' remembers Col Yashwant Singh Rawat, who is to lead his company in the attack. Maj. Kelkar seems quiet and withdrawn. Then, all of a sudden, he asks, '*Maj. Prem Das ki death kaise hui thi?*' Maj. Das was the former second-in-command of the battalion who had been killed during the 1965 war.

Kelkar is told that while the entire battalion had gone on attack, Maj. Das had been asked to stay back in the battalion headquarters. He was in his bunker, and since he had nothing to do, he had summoned the unit barber and decided to get a haircut. Two Sabre jets returning from an unsuccessful mission saw the brigade vehicles parked below and decided to empty their arsenal on that spot instead of taking it back to Pakistan. They dropped napalm bombs and the entire area went up in flames. Maj. Das was burnt to death. Kelkar then wants to know, 'How did Major Thomson [another second-in-command] die?'

'I think he was remembering the jinx that seconds-in-command seemed to have, since we had lost so many of them, and he had some kind of premonition about his own future,' Col Rawat remembers.

The premonition does come true. It so happens that during the battle, an enemy bullet comes and hits Major Kelkar's helmet, knocking it off. A second bullet hits him in the head, and he loses his life in the battlefield. Maj. Ian Cardozo, the next second-in-command of the unit, also steps on a mine and has his leg blown off. Superstitious troops asked the CO to start calling the second-in-command of the unit 'Vazir' to break this terrible jinx, and that has been followed ever since.

A Box of Sweets

16 December 1971
0130 hours
Jarpal (23 km inside Pakistan)

The victorious Sikh officer stands in the battlefield, tall and proud. He wears a battered steel helmet over his *patka*. Around him the land burns, and bodies lie scattered. What should have been the quietest hours of the night are punctured by screams of shells and moans of men injured or dying. Though Jarpal has been conquered, at other locations the battle still rages.

Soldiers of both sides have paid the price for the bloody conflict. Maj. Satvinder Singh Cheema, commander, Bravo Company, 3 Grenadiers, is surveying the devastation. His head is held high but his eyes are tinged with sadness for comrades lost. A captured Pakistani soldier is bending down in front of him, his khaki uniform dirty, his trousers soaked in blood. He is trying to touch Cheema's feet. 'Don't do that,' Cheema snaps. 'Maintain the dignity of the uniform you and I wear.' His voice is colder than the chilly winter wind lashing their faces. The enemy soldier scrambles to his feet.

Just about an hour back, Cheema had looked at his watch. The time had been 0030 hours, half an hour past midnight. Breathless from battle, he had picked up the radio set and called his commanding officer, Lieutenant Colonel V.P. Airy. 'Sukh,' he had said. A smile had spread across the anxiously waiting Col Airy's face. 'Sukh' was the success signal chosen by Cheema. It was short for 'Sukhinder'. Tall, slim Sukhinder with the big eyes. Ever-smiling. Ever concerned about his welfare. Gentle and soft-spoken. With a loving wife. Today, 16 December, was her birthday too. He had celebrated with live fireworks. Pakistan's 24 Punjab had been decimated and Jarpal was now theirs.

A Few Hours Back

The night of 15–16 December 1971
2230 hours
Basantar nala, Zafarwal sector
Pakistan

The night is dark and chilly. Across the shadowy sugar cane and wheat fields that the soldiers of 3 Grenadiers have already crossed flows the Basantar nala. The water is not in spate and has a gentle white glow in the moonlight. The tranquillity of the nala is disturbed only by the splashing caused by boot-clad feet stepping into it.

Looking at the nala's sublime stillness, no one can guess just how frigid it is. This sinks in for the soldiers only after they step into it and the wetness seeps into their leather boots and socks, pricking their soles like hundreds of sharp needles.

More than 120 men of Charlie Company (led by Maj. Hoshiar Singh) and 120 of Bravo Company (led by Maj. S.S. Cheema) are wading across the river, oblivious to its beauty and, to an extent, even its freezing temperatures. What concerns them more is the near-constant shelling and machine-gun fire directed right into their faces, and the minefields that they know the Pakistanis have laid out on the other side, which they will have to cross to reach their destination. The two companies have been tasked with attacking and capturing Jarpal from the east and west respectively, around midnight.

In their jackets, helmets and ankle boots, the soldiers splash across the freezing water in silence. Their faces are smeared with mud and gunpowder from the shelling they have endured. Every time the water lashes their skin it feels like a knife is cutting into their flesh. After a while their exposed bodies go numb but the men trudge on, the water coming up to their knees, their weapons held high above their heads, away from the water. The soldiers carry 7.62 mm rifles and Sten guns, while the radio operators accompanying them have their pistols. Each man is carrying at least two grenades. Close combat is expected.

Cheema is watching his men cross the nala, a worried frown creasing his forehead. He doesn't want any accidents.

His wet trousers are flapping around his legs, making goosepimples erupt on his skin. The map of Jarpal is stamped on to his mind. His task is to attack in the dark; the enemy has to be taken unawares. Unfortunately, though, they can make out nothing in the distance except a dense green cover. Col Airy has told him to keep going—'*Naak ki seedh mein*'—and that is what he plans to do.

Just before the two companies moved away from the battalion location, Col Airy had hugged both his young company commanders leading the attack and wished them the best. In that emotional moment, none of them knew how many would come back alive.

After crossing the nala, the two companies separate. Cheema knows it is going to be a long night. What he does not know yet is that his company will be in the thick of one of the fiercest battles ever fought by the Indian Army.

~

Cheema's eyes look tired and sleep-deprived but they breathe fire. He is looking at his POW in disgust. 'Stand up and talk to me as one soldier talks to another,' he says, his voice sharp though steeped in fatigue.

Behind him stand his radio operator and a few of the braves of Bravo Company. Their clothes are ripped from crawling around while digging the trenches they will take shelter in for the night since counterattacks are expected. Their pants are still wet from wading across the Basantar nala, and their nerves raw from dodging enemy land mines and MMG fire. Though victory has kissed their feet, their hearts are weighed down with the memories of friends they used to joke around with—who now lie dead in the fields with vacant eyes staring into oblivion.

The nasty, ear-splitting scream of an enemy shell pierces the air. For a fraction of a second, it lights up the frightened face of the Pakistani rifleman whom they have found injured in a grenade attack and have already disarmed. He is pleading for his life.

'*Tussi meri ek gal tey sun lo, sahab*,' the Pakistani soldier cries out piteously. Grenade splinters have cut deep into his flesh and he is weak from loss of blood. Something in his voice makes Cheema stop. '*Mera bachcha bahut beemar rehta hai, meri biwi padhi likhi nahi hai. Mere alawa unko dekhne wala koi nahi hai, sahab. Mere bina wo dono mar jaayenge*,' the man is saying. '*Mainu chad do, sahab.*'

'*Aye mai kaar nahi sakda*,' the major replies curtly in Punjabi, 'You are a POW and I cannot let you go.' He turns to his radio operator. 'Tie him up and put him with the others,' he says.

~

Cheema and his men are tired and hungry. They have spent the night crawling around, surviving on rationed water drunk sip by precious sip from fast-depleting stocks in their water bottles. Their trousers are caked with mud and dried blood. Their faces are stained with grime and gunfire. This is not the time to relax. Counter-attacks are sure to come.

'*Sahab, meri gal tey sun lo tussi,*' the enemy soldier is pleading again. 'You have won the battle. We have lost. I am just another enemy soldier. My life means nothing to you but it means the world to my family. You have made so many prisoners, one less will make no difference to you, but if you let me go, it will mean the difference between life and death to my family.' He is fumbling for words. Cheema looks at his watch. The time is 0200 hours. The Pakistanis are probably planning a counter-attack to take back their land. He and his men have to be prepared.

Cheema decides that enough time has been lost. He turns to go, his eyes signalling to his soldiers to do the needful. His arm swings and his right hand goes habitually to the Gutka Sahib (a breviary containing chosen *banis* from Sikh scriptures) he always carries in his side pack. It has been with him since he was a young boy—he had even carried it to the 1965 war. '*Meri jaan baksh do, sahab,*' the Pakistani soldier's desperate voice reaches his ears. Fingertips lingering over the raised contours of the breviary pressing against the rough fabric of his haversack, Cheema turns around.

'*Theek hai*!' he says. 'I will let you go, but only on one condition. I shall count till ten. If you can disappear by then, you are free. But if you are still in the range of my rifle, I shall shoot you.' The Pakistani soldier nods. Cheema takes a rifle from one of his soldiers. Aiming it at the soldier, he says, '*Chal bhag! Main ginti shuru kar reha hun. Sharat yaad raakhi.*'

'*Aapka ehsaan zindagi bhar nahi bhulunga, sahab,*' the prisoner cries out, hope writ large upon his frightened face.

Wiping the tears staining his dry, sallow cheeks, he stands at attention and salutes Cheema, who stands grimly, rifle in hand. And then, the POW turns around and starts to run. '*Ek*.' Cheema's voice is loud and clear. The enemy soldier fumbles, his legs buckling under his weight. '*Do*.' He picks himself up clumsily and starts shuffling away. Cheema is counting as slowly as he can. '*Teen*.' The man is pulling his injured leg behind him as he drags himself forward.

'*Chaar . . . paanch*.'

He can hear the click of the rifle. A bullet has fallen into place.

'*Chhe*.'

The man is sweating in the freezing cold as he tries to limp ahead as fast as he can.

'*Saat*.'

'*Aath*.'

'*Nau*.'

The released prisoner is now too far away to hear Cheema's words in the din of gunfire, but try as hard as he can, he cannot run. He has lost too much blood, his body is racked with pain, the splinters in his leg are cutting like blades at every step, and his mouth is dry and parched. The best he can do is crawl. The Indian soldiers watch nervously.

Cheema has a resigned look on his face. A vein throbs in his neck. A shell erupts again, lighting up the sky like daylight. The man is in his sights, pushing himself forward, holding his injured leg with both hands, and leaving behind a trail of blood in the dry mud. Cheema closes an eye and takes aim. He looks emotionlessly at the frail soldier in khaki desperately trying to drag himself towards safety and his loved ones. '*Dus*,' Cheema counts, a note of finality in his voice. And then he lifts the borrowed 7.62 and pulls the trigger.

Turning around with the rifle still smoking, he orders his men to the trenches and tells them to be prepared. Later that day and the morning after, Pakistan's 35 Frontier Force launches around seven counter-attacks to reoccupy Jarpal, but all of these are beaten back by the men of Bravo and Charlie companies. The Pakistanis suffer heavy casualties. A few hours later, Indira Gandhi declares a ceasefire. On 17 December 1971, both sides stop firing and the war is officially over.

A Few Months Later

Jarpal
April 1972

The soldiers continue to live in trenches. They are awaiting orders. Talks are going on between the two governments but no decision has yet been arrived at with regard to pulling out the armies. Cheema has come back from leave after meeting his wife and children—their three-year-old daughter and their son, who is only one year old and has started taking his first wobbly steps.

A soldier walks up to him. '*Jai Hind, sahab! Aapse koi milna chahta hai*,' he says, pointing in the distance to a man in khaki. Beside him is a pencil-thin woman in salwar kameez, a dupatta draped over her head, covering most of her face. She is holding on to the hand of a small child. Cheema squints into the bright morning sunshine. 'Who are they?' he wonders, walking towards the visitors. The man steps forward with a smile and salutes him smartly.

Cheema looks at him. '*Kaun ho aap*?' he asks.

'*Sahab, tussi mainu pachaniya nahi*?' the Pakistani soldier asks.

'*Nahi*,' Cheema replies. And then, an old memory flashes in front of his eyes. Of an injured soldier in a bloodied uniform, weeping tears of frustration, trying to drag himself to freedom. 'Oye!' he calls out. '*Tu oi hai jinu sat lagi si*?' he asks, his brow creased as he tries to remember the man's face.

'*Hanji, sahab, main ohi han*,' the released POW replies.

'You survived your wounds!' Cheema is incredulous. 'I didn't think you would live.'

The Pakistani soldier's eyes are moist. '*Zakhm te gehre si per bach gaya, sahab*,' he says. '*Aapki meherbani hai.*'

'*Rab di meherbani hai*,' Cheema replies, leaning forward to hug the enemy soldier. It feels like he has been reunited with a loved one.

'I have got something for you, sahab, please don't say no,' says the soldier, holding out a box of sweets. '*Wo dekho, sahab, wo meri biwi hai. Usne ye mithai bhijwai hai aapke liye. Saath mei mera bachcha khada hai. Uski tabiyat ab theek hai, sahab. Dono aapka shukriya ada karne aaye hain. Jab tak ham zinda hain aapka ehsaan nahi bhulenge*,' the man says, pointing to his family.

Courtesy: Damayanti Tambay's personal album

Flt Lt Vijay Vasant Tambay and Damayanti. They spent a brief but happy span together.

Damayanti Tambay at seventy-two: Still looking for answers about what happened to her missing husband.

Courtesy: Damayanti Tambay's personal album

The author with Damayanti Tambay at her flat in Munirka Vihar, New Delhi.

Reproduced from *Missing in Action* by Chander Suta Dogra, with permission from HarperCollins India

Scan of a *Time* magazine article dated 27 December 1971 that has a picture of two Indian POWs looking through the bars of a prison cell in Pakistan. The one in front bears an uncanny resemblance to Maj. Ashok Kumar Ghosh, missing in action. Damayanti Tambay believes that the man behind him is her husband, Flt Lt Vijay Tambay, also missing in action.

Flt Lt Vijay Vasant Tambay.

Reproduced from *Missing in Action*

Reproduced from *Missing in Action*

Maj. Ashok Kumar Ghosh.

Courtesy: Air Cmde Jawahar Lal Bhargava

Repatriated POWs arriving back in India.

Courtesy: Air Cmde Jawahar Lal Bhargava

Flying Officer Jawahar Lal Bhargava getting his wings on 9 March 1963.

Air Cmde Jawahar Lal Bhargava

The man who brazenly tried to pass himself off as Flt Lt Mansoor Ali Khan.

Air Cmde Jawahar Lal Bhargava

The best pilot of his time.

Courtesy: Air Cmde Jawahar Lal Bhargava

Living with memories: Air Cmde Bhargava at his Panchkula home.

Courtesy: Late Brig. A.B. Harolikar's personal album, through Jaya Harolikar

Company Commanders of 4/5 Gorkha Rifles on their way to Atgram. (*Left to right*): Maj. Dinesh Singh Rana, Maj. Ratan Kaul, Maj. Yashwant Singh Rawat (*without cap*), Maj. Man Mohan Malik (*standing in front*).

Officers of 4/5 GR with captured enemy weapons. Capt. D.K. Sen Gupta, SM, is the man in spectacles (*second from right*).

Courtesy: Late Brig. A.B. Harolikar's personal album

Courtesy: Late Brig. A.B. Harolikar's personal album

Lt Gen. A.S. Arora meets Naik Dil Bahadur Chhetri, MVC, while CO Lt Col A.B. Harolikar looks on.

Courtesy: Late Brig. A.B. Harolikar's personal album

Dil Bahadur Chhetri, MVC, with Gen. S.H.F.J. Manekshaw, MC.

Prime Minister Indira Gandhi flanked by Lt Col Arun Bhimrao Harolikar (*left*) and Lt Col Amarjit Singh Brar (*right*), along with their wives.

Courtesy: Late Brig. A.B. Harolikar's personal album

Courtesy: Late Brig. A.B. Harolikar's personal album

Lt Col Arun Bhimrao Harolikar with General Sam Manekshaw.

Lt Col A.B. Harolikar, MVC, meeting Prime Minister Indira Gandhi.

Courtesy: Late Brig. A.B. Harolikar's personal album

Courtesy: Late Brig. A.B. Harolikar's personal album

Naik Dil Bahadur Chhetri, MVC.

Courtesy: Late Brig. A.B. Harolikar's personal album

Rifleman Phas Bahadur Pun, VrC (posthumous)

Courtesy: Late Brig. A.B. Harolikar's personal album

2/Lt Hawa Singh, VrC (posthumous).

Courtesy: Late Brig. A.B. Harolikar's personal album

Capt. P.K. Johri, SM (posthumous).

Courtesy: Late Brig. A.B. Harolikar's personal album

Sub. Tirtha Bahadur Gurung, SM.

Members of the One-Legged Club: (*Left to right, standing*) Maj. Kipgen of the Assam Regt, Maj. Gen. Ian Cardozo, (*bottom left, seated*) Maj. Abu Tahir of the Bangladesh Army and (*bottom right*) Col Y.S. Rawat.

The late Maj. S.G. Kelkar, Vazir.

Courtesy: Col Cheema's personal album

A picture taken after the Battle of Jarpal, with Col Hoshiar Singh and Col S.S. Cheema still in battle gear.

Lt Col K.S. Pannu shaking hands with the enemy commander at Mirpur. 2 Para was the first unit of the Indian Army to enter Dacca.

Courtesy: Col Lali Gill

Courtesy: Col Lali Gill.

The young paratrooper Lali Gill during a desert exercise in 1979.

The young officer Lali getting a taste of a soldier's life.

Courtesy: Col Lali Gill

Courtesy: Dr David Muthumani

Dr David Muthumani.

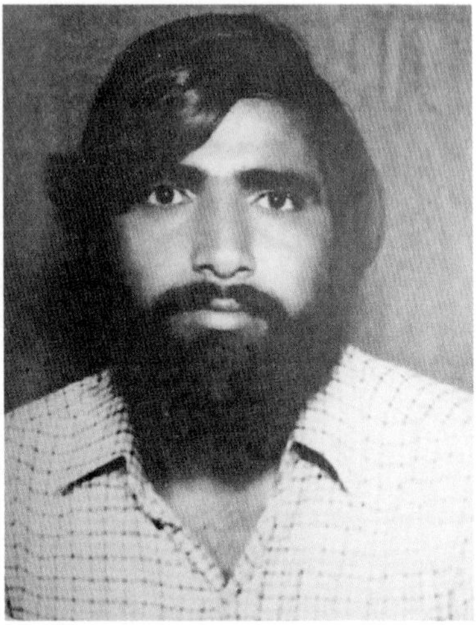

Courtesy: PO Chiman Singh

Petty Officer Chiman Singh Yadav, MVC, in a picture taken in October 1971.

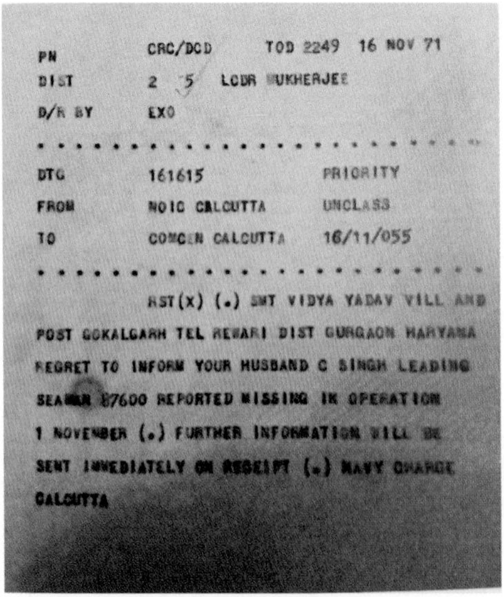

PN CRC/DCD TOD 2249 16 NOV 71
DIST 2 5 LCDR MUKHERJEE
D/R BY EXO
. . . .
DTG 161615 PRIORITY
FROM NOIC CALCUTTA UNCLASS
TO COMCEN CALCUTTA 16/11/055
. . . .
RST(X) (.) SMT VIDYA YADAV VILL AND
POST GOKALGARH TEL REWARI DIST GURGAON HARYANA
REGRET TO INFORM YOUR HUSBAND C SINGH LEADING
SEAMAN 87600 REPORTED MISSING IN OPERATION
1 NOVEMBER (.) FURTHER INFORMATION WILL BE
SENT IMMEDIATELY ON RECEIPT (.) NAVY CHARGE
CALCUTTA

Courtesy: PO Chiman Singh

The message received by PO Chiman Singh's wife when he went missing in November 1971.

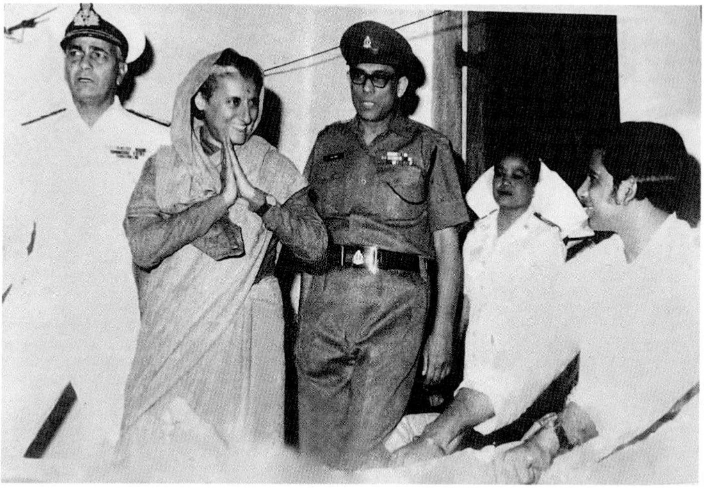

Prime Minister Indira Gandhi visiting a hospitalized Chiman Singh.

PO Chiman Singh receiving the MVC from President V.V. Giri.

A proud Petty Officer Chiman Singh Yadav, now retired and settled in his village in Haryana, with his Maha Vir Chakra.

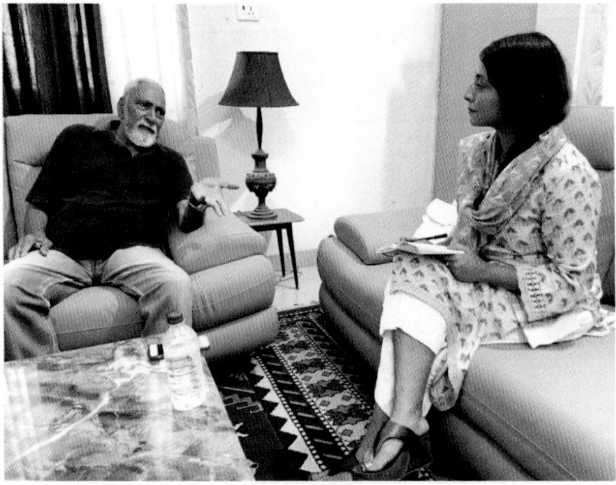

The author interviewing PO Chiman Singh at his farmhouse in Gokalgarh village, Haryana.

Courtesy: Mukesh Khetarpal

2/Lt Arun Khetarpal, PVC.

Courtesy: Mukesh Khetarpal

Arun Khetarpal during his training at the National Defence Academy.

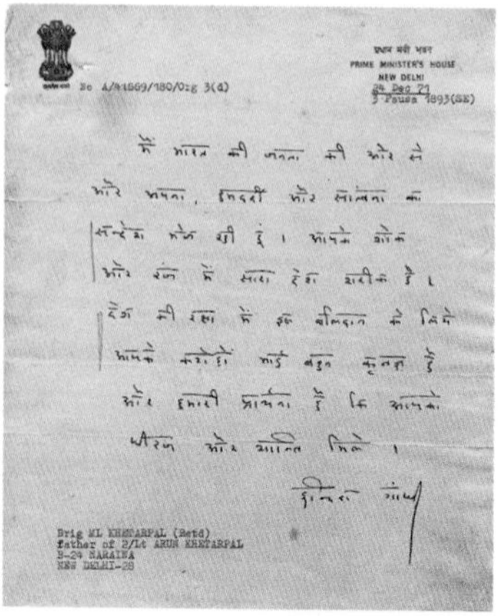

प्रधान मंत्री भवन
PRIME MINISTER'S HOUSE
NEW DELHI
24 Dec 71
3 Pausa 1893(SE)

No A/41669/180/Org 3(d)

मैं भारत की जनता की ओर से और अपनी, हमदर्दी और सांत्वना का सन्देश भेज रही हूं। आपके शोक और दुःख में सारा देश शरीक है। देश की रक्षा में इस बलिदान के लिये आपके करोड़ों भाई बहुत कृतज्ञ हैं और हमारी प्रार्थना है कि आपको धीरज और शान्ति मिले।

इन्दिरा गांधी

Brig ML KHETARPAL (Retd)
father of 2/Lt ARUN KHETARPAL
B-24 NARAINA
NEW DELHI-28

Courtesy: Mukesh Khetarpal

A handwritten condolence letter from Prime Minister Indira Gandhi to Brig. M.L. Khetarpal.

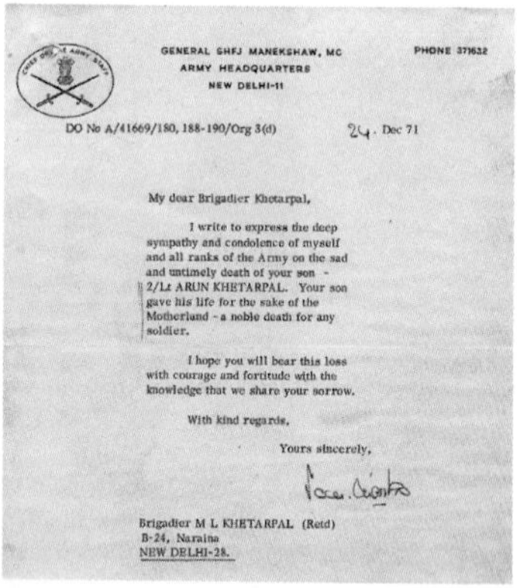

GENERAL SHFJ MANEKSHAW, MC
ARMY HEADQUARTERS
NEW DELHI-11

PHONE 371632

DO No A/41669/180, 188-190/Org 3(d) 24. Dec 71

My dear Brigadier Khetarpal,

I write to express the deep sympathy and condolence of myself and all ranks of the Army on the sad and untimely death of your son - 2/Lt ARUN KHETARPAL. Your son gave his life for the sake of the Motherland - a noble death for any soldier.

I hope you will bear this loss with courage and fortitude with the knowledge that we share your sorrow.

With kind regards,

Yours sincerely,

Brigadier M L KHETARPAL (Retd)
B-24, Naraina
NEW DELHI-28.

A moving note from COAS Gen. Sam Manekshaw, MC, to Brig. M.L. Khetarpal.

Courtesy: Mukesh Khetarpal

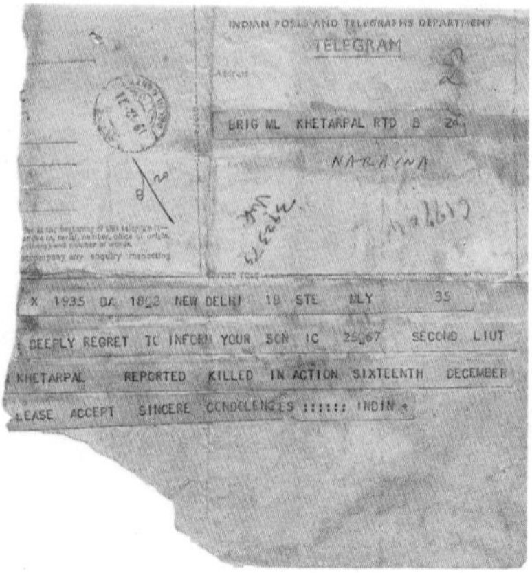

INDIAN POSTS AND TELEGRAPHS DEPARTMENT
TELEGRAM

BRIG ML KHETARPAL RTD B 24
NARAINA

X 1935 DA 1802 NEW DELHI 19 STE DLY 35
DEEPLY REGRET TO INFORM YOUR SON IC 25067 SECOND LIUT
KHETARPAL REPORTED KILLED IN ACTION SIXTEENTH DECEMBER
PLEASE ACCEPT SINCERE CONDOLENCES :::::: INDIN +

Courtesy: Mukesh Khetarpal

Telegram received by Brig. M.L. Khetarpal informing him about his son 2/Lt Arun Khetarpal's sacrifice in the battlefield.

Courtesy: Mukesh Khetarpal

Brig M.L. Khetarpal with Brig. Khwaja Mohammad Naser in Lahore.

Courtesy: Col Sajjad

Col Sajjad with Param Vir Chakra awardee Lance Naik Albert Ekka's widow, Balamdina, and son, Vincent.

Courtesy: Brig. D.S. Adhikari

Capt. D.S. Adhikari sitting with his men in the captured enemy trenches.

Courtesy: Brig. D.S. Adhikari

Capt. D.S. Adhikari with his commanding officer, Lt Col K.C. Tiwari, and some of the captured weapons.

Courtesy: Brig. D.S. Adhikari

Capt. D.S. Adhikari (*first from right*) being introduced to Gen. Sam Manekshaw immediately after the war.

Cheema opens the box. It holds a layer of rich, creamy barfi. Taking out a piece, Cheema breaks it in two, placing one half in the enemy soldier's mouth and eating the other half himself. He then returns the box. '*Shukriya! Main kha lai, baki sab nu khua dena*,' he says, his voice gruff with emotion. The Pakistani soldier wipes off tears with the back of his hand and walks away. Cheema watches him go. He can see the lady in salwar kameez dropping to her knees and touching her forehead to the ground in a *sajda*. The child has lifted his right arm in a salute. Cheema stands at attention and returns the salute. His hand instinctively moves to the Gutka Sahib still in his pocket. He remembers how he had deliberately fired a shot above the retreating enemy soldier's head four months ago. 'Waheguru! Never allow me to shoot a man in the back,' he whispers to himself.

Far away somewhere, from some masjid in Pakistan, snatches of the azan carry in the wind and spread over the trenches. Cheema's lips move silently to the prayer that his own religion has taught him. '*Ik onkar. Satnam. Karta purakh. Nirbhau. Nirvair. Akaal moorat* (There is only one God. His name is true. He is the creator. He has no fear. He has no hate. He is omnipresent),' he whispers to himself, slowly walking back to where his soldiers stand watching.

Author's Note

In December 1971, 3 Grenadiers was told to open the front for 54 Division in the western sector where they were deployed. Their first attack took place on the night of 5 December when they captured the Bhairavnath temple area and were then moved to protect the flank of 54 Division at a place called Narainpur Dinga, Fatehpur Beri.

On 15 December, the unit was tasked with attacking Jarpal, a heavily defended village about 23 km inside Pakistan. Maj. (later Col) S.S. Cheema and Maj. (later Col) Hoshiar Singh, who went on to win the Param Vir Chakra for that operation, were young company commanders in the unit, and both were so eager to face action on that fateful day that they sat with bated breath when their CO Col (later Lt Gen.) V.P. Airy announced which companies would be attacking Jarpal. 'Hoshiar and I were sitting next to each other,' Col Cheema remembers. 'He turned to me and said he was going to be really upset if his company was not included in the attack. I told him if my company was not picked up I would go and have it out with the CO!'

When Col Airy disclosed the attack plan, the two officers looked at each other and smiled. Both companies had been picked for phase one of the attack.

This story is based on an interview with Col S.S. Cheema (retd), Sena Medal, who later went on to command 3 Grenadiers. He now lives in Jalandhar.

Bloodied in Tangail

11 December 1971
0500 hours
Dum Dum Airport
Calcutta

A boxy-looking military aircraft waits at the runway, ready to take paratroopers to war. It is a two-doored Fairchild C-119 Boxcar—popularly called Packet in the Indian Army.

Meanwhile, in a dark, deserted hangar, a lone light bulb dangles at the end of a long cable. Swaying slightly in the draught coming in from the open door, it spills a quivering circle of yellow light that falls on a Sikh soldier standing on top of a dusty wooden stool with a parachute on his back. It illuminates the rugged contours of his face. Young, handsome, bearded, with a steel helmet strapped under his chin, he has sweat on his brow even in the December cold. On one shoulder hangs his carbine. In front, his knapsack containing a change of clothes, his ammunition, grenades and food (dry puris and shakkarparas rolled up in a piece of newspaper).

Twenty-one-year-old 2nd Lt Lalinder Jit Singh Gill from Charlie Company, 2nd Battalion, the Parachute Regiment, is going to war with his battalion. The paratroopers shall be airdropped inside East Pakistan. Since Lali has joined his unit straight from the Indian Military Academy (IMA), he has not received any para training. He is being taught how to jump from a plane and has about twenty minutes to learn.

A nervous Lali shuffles his feet, his heavy DMS (direct moulded sole) boots making the rickety old stool creak. '*Seedhe khade raho, sahab*,' snaps Sgt Lakhan Pal. A sturdy, no-nonsense Jat, he is pacing impatiently in front of Lali, his face dark and scowling. Lali's eyes seek Flt Lt Banerjee, the third man in the hangar, who stands by watching nonchalantly.

'So you haven't done your para probation?' Banerjee drawls.

'No, sir.'

'Ever been inside a plane?'

'No, sir.'

'When did you join the battalion?'

'Ten days back, sir,' an apologetic Lali stutters nervously.

'And you want to go to war?'

This time there is no hesitation in the youngster's voice. 'Yes, sir,' he says, his voice steeped in steely determination.

Banerjee rolls his eyes and leaves the hangar.

Lakhan Pal is the man appointed to give Lali a crash course in para jumping. He has already gone over the basics. How to sit, how to stand, how to exit the plane, what to do when the parachute opens (or doesn't) and how to hit the ground with minimum impact. Now it is time for the practical.

'Jump,' Lakhan Pal shouts, his booming voice echoing in the vacant recesses of the hangar. Lali leaps off the stool, hitting the ground with knees bent, and rolls over on the dirty floor. Face and hands stained with grime, he quickly gets up and stands at attention to anxiously face his instructor. There is a half-smile on Lakhan Pal's scarred face. '*Shabash*!' he says. '*Ab aise hi ladai ke maidan mein bhi kudega. Aur zinda wapis aayega*!' With that the class is dismissed. Lali scrambles out into the breaking orange dawn to join the other paratroopers who are making the most of the free time by grabbing some sleep. Most lie sprawled, heads resting on rolled-up parachutes. Lali dumps his packs and spreads out on the floor.

~

June 2021
Mohali

Col Lali Gill is seventy-one now. It has been nearly fifty years since the day he stood on a stool in that deserted Calcutta hangar, but he says it still feels like yesterday. Having retired from service, he normally spends his time globetrotting between Chandigarh and Switzerland, where his daughter is married to a local resident. This year, however, the proud paratrooper has been restricted to his Mohali house because of the COVID-induced lockdown. He very graciously gives me time for an interview, sharing with me his priceless memories, photographs from the battle, old articles and war records. He helps me time-travel back to the December of 1971 when his battalion had been earmarked to airdrop inside enemy territory for a daredevil operation that only the paratroopers would have the gumption to attempt.

He begins telling me his extraordinary story from the day he reached Calcutta to join his battalion, just fifteen days after having graduated from the Indian Military Academy.

~

29 November 1971
1600 hours
Howrah Junction Railway Station

Amid the cacophony of tea vendors, passengers and coolies in red scurrying around with suitcases and hold-alls balanced on their heads, there is the piercing scream of a train horn. The Kalka Express screams into the platform and slowly shudders to a halt. One of the first persons to jump out is a young Sikh second lieutenant with shining eyes and rugged good looks. Smartly attired in a well-fitted olive-green uniform, slightly crushed from his journey from Chandigarh, he stands tall at 6'1". He is dragging behind him a black wooden box, neatly stencilled '2Lt L.J.S. Gill, Indian Military Academy, Dehradun to Calcutta'.

It doesn't take 2 PARA's Subedar Govind Jadhav, who is waiting at the platform, much time to spot the '*naya sahab*' who has come to join the unit. The stocky JCO steps forward with a smile. '*Jai Hind, sahab. Paltan mein aapka swagat hai*,' he says, saluting crisply. Lali salutes back. He has opted to join the parachute regiment after graduating from IMA's 48 Regular course. The course's graduation, that had originally been scheduled for 21 December, has been moved ahead by six weeks since the country is going to war and the army needs gutsy young officers. Lali is bristling to see action.

~

Nostalgia seeps into Col Gill's deep, grainy voice. 'Jadhav drove me down to the unit location at Botanical Gardens. I found it strange that the area was heavily guarded. That was when he told me that the unit was earmarked for an airborne operation and had been placed in quarantine. No one was allowed to interact with anyone outside the camp to ensure complete secrecy about the impending operation. I was put up in a forty-pounder tent on the banks of the Hooghly.'

~

On the morning of 1 December, Lali is started off on a twenty-eight-day para probation with the Charlie Company commander Maj. J.S. Mahalwar as his probation officer.

Mahalwar tells the crestfallen Lali that though the battalion is going to war, he (Lali) will not be accompanying the unit since he is not a trained paratrooper yet.

Lali goes looking for his CO, the dashing Col (later Maj. Gen.) Kulwant Singh Pannu, and finds him smoking a cigarette. 'Sir, I want to go to war too,' he says. Col Pannu blows a smoke ring in the air. 'Sorry, son, you can't come. You have never jumped before in your life,' he answers.

Not one to give up easily, Lali carries on. 'Everybody jumps for the first time once, sir,' he says, desperation writ large upon his young face. 'Why can't my first jump be in the battlefield?'

Pannu watches through narrowed eyes. He doesn't say a word. Lali returns to his tent twirling his jungle cap around a finger. An optimist at heart, he is happy that he hasn't been turned down.

That same evening, 50 Para Brigade commander Brig. (later Lt Gen.) Mathew Thomas, a short, stocky, confident man, drives down to the 2 PARA location along with some of his officers. He has come to boost the unit's morale. A basketball match is scheduled where the brigade commander himself plays, though his team is beaten by the home team. Lali, the newest addition to the unit, who happens to be an ace basketball player, is brought forth and introduced to the brigade commander. 'This youngster hasn't done his para probation but he wants to come with us to war, sir,' Col Pannu tells him as a nervous Lali watches.

Thomas smiles indulgently. 'And what will I tell your father if something goes wrong, young fellow?' he asks, an arm resting on the young lieutenant's shoulder.

'Sir, tell him what you would tell any other soldier's father if something were to go wrong with them,' he replies earnestly.

Brig. Thomas looks at Col Pannu. 'Okay!' he says, shrugging his shoulders. 'He can go.' He moves on to meet the other soldiers.

The decision shocks everyone. None of the company commanders want Lali since he is untrained, and bringing him along on an operation is a risk that no one wants to take. Finally, Lali's probation officer, Major Mahalwar, agrees to take him into Charlie Company.

~

9 December 1971
Botanical Gardens

There is excitement in the camp. The much-awaited battle orders have come. On 11 December, the battalion will be flown inside enemy territory and dropped at a place called Tangail in East Pakistan. The paratroopers will attack and capture Poongli, a bridge on the Louhajang River that flows nearby and separates Dacca, the capital of East Pakistan, from the rest of the land. The move is aimed at blocking Pakistan's 93rd Brigade (that is being thrashed by the Indian forces in a place called Mymensingh up north) from retreating to Dacca.

The attack plan is formulated. The first to be dropped inside enemy territory shall be Charlie Company. The paratroopers shall jump from Dakota C-47s which would lift off from Kalaikunda—a fighter base a few hours' drive from Calcutta. Their task would be to secure the forming-up place (FUP), a piece of ground from where the attacking companies will launch. At approximately the same time, Packet aircraft, taking off from Dum Dum Airport, would drop off two groups, Pathfinder 1 and 2, at the Tangail dropping zone (DZ). They would be responsible for marking the DZ and receiving the attacking companies. Alfa and Bravo, the two attacking companies, would be the last to jump, also to be carried by the Packets.

The single-doored Dakota C-47 is considered a technically complex aircraft to jump from (particularly for first-timers) because strong wind currents tend to push against jumping paratroopers and heighten the risk of injury or getting hung from the plane. Lali is assigned to Pathfinder 2, to be dropped by the Packet, a relatively simpler aircraft to jump from.

~

11 December 1971
1600 hours

The Packet flies over Tangail. It carries a full load of forty-one paratroopers, kitted up with their 20 kg load of main and reserve parachutes, weapons and ammunition. A nervous

Lali is last in line, his heart thumping so loud that he fears others might be able to hear it too. Fear is mingled with excitement since this is his first time on a plane.

The warning hooter sounds and, five minutes to the jump, the red light starts flashing. The men stand and hook up to their parachute static line. The doors open, blowing a strong gust of wind into their faces. Moving forward, they start dropping off one by one from the two doors at the rear of the aircraft.

Lali finally reaches the door. He has already told the air force staff that he is not to be pushed. 'I will jump myself,' he has said, trying to keep his voice confident. Inside, his nerves are in a complete tangle. The cold December wind whips his face like a lash. Down below, he can see an unending expanse of blue with the paratroopers who have jumped off showing as fading dots in the sky.

As the red light at the door turns green, Lakhan Pal's voice rings out in his head. '*Hare pe kudega.*' Taking a deep breath, Lali steels his nerves and takes a leap of faith.

~

Falling through the air at breakneck speed, Lali feels a massive jerk in his back and legs. He looks up to find green fabric unfurling above his head and billowing in the wind. His parachute has opened. Floating in the air, he is filled with a tremendous sense of relief. He has done it and he is still alive!

~

A smile spills across the grand old man's face as he remembers his first jump. 'It took me a minute to reach the ground from 1250 feet. Looking down, I could see a flat brown patch rushing up at me and felt really fortunate that I was getting a smooth, grassy tabletop to land on,' he recollects.

It is only when his feet hit ice-cold water that rushes up to engulf his body that Lali realizes he has fallen into water. 'I just sank into the pond and when I emerged, water was lapping around me up to my shoulders. It was freezing cold but at least I didn't get hurt.' Col Gill laughs, going on to describe the stinking muck that covered him as he waded through the water. 'It was a very bad landing,' he admits, 'but I was filled with a deep sense of achievement. I was elated that I could jump with my battalion in the war zone.'

Walking out of the pond, Lali unharnesses himself. His ammunition, weapon, kit, blanket, food, parachute and clothes are soaked. Rolling up his wet parachute, he sprints towards the DZ that is 800 m away where everybody else has landed, his wet shoes squirting water at each step. He is greeted with a volley of abuse from Pathfinder 2 commander, Maj. P.L. Tiwari. 'He gave me a piece of his mind for drifting away, for falling into water and also for carrying my parachute since I had forgotten instructions that it was to be dumped at the place of landing,' Col Gill remembers. By then, Pathfinder 1 has already secured the DZ and put up lights for the main body, and the mainstream paratroopers have started dropping from the sky. Packets and Dakotas fly past. The sky is filled with black dots that slowly turn into olive-green parachutes, and young paratroopers start landing on the ground one after the other. After unhooking their parachutes, they sprint to the FUP. Eight recoilless (RCL) and six artillery guns are also dropped with the soldiers.

In what will be remembered in the history of the parachute regiment as a crafty and shrewd battle move, Caribou aircraft are used to drop dummy loads at the same time in various locations. This confuses the enemy, leading it to believe that an entire brigade (three battalions or 1800 men) is landing at Tangail, whereas only one battalion of around 600 men has landed.

~

At 2000 hours, Alfa and Bravo companies get attack orders. When the two companies and the CO's party reach the bridge, they are surprised to find it deserted. Completely fooled by the dummy drops by the aircraft and terrorized by what they believe is a massive landing of enemy paratroopers, the Pakistanis have fled. Peering down from the bridge, the soldiers spot some moving lights in the darkness. They quickly identify it as a convoy of enemy vehicles heading in their direction. The Pakistani forces are fleeing to Dacca since they have been beaten by the Indian Army at Jamalpur, 80 km away.

Col Pannu orders the men to get down from the bridge and take on the enemy soldiers before they reach it. Bravo Company is placed on the left side of the road while Alfa Company is on the Tangail side. The paratroopers take cover in the foliage and watch the headlights of the enemy convoy slowly come closer. The moment the vehicles are in firing range, Paratrooper Vaidya Nath Shinge, who is balancing a rocket launcher on his shoulder, fires at the one-and-a-half-tonner lumbering along. The truck goes up in the air and rolls on to the other side, catching fire. It turns turtle and lies there burning with its wheels in the air. Orange flames lick the cold December air lighting up the road. The Pakistanis are shocked to find armed paratroopers emerging from behind the shrubs on both sides. A fierce battle rages through the night.

A Pakistani captain gets a bullet in his butt and is captured alive. He is taken to the battalion headquarters, his uniform filthy and bloodstained. 'I have been shot,' he tells Col Pannu. 'Could I get a cigarette?' Col Pannu holds out his own pack to the injured officer. The captain draws out a cigarette with trembling fingers. Pannu leans forward to light it for him and then one for himself. The two share a smoke in silence for a while and then start talking. After all details of the battle situation have been extracted from him, the Pakistani officer is operated upon by the 2 PARA mobile medical team and the bullet is removed.

Meanwhile, in the battlefield, there is complete chaos. Many of the Pakistani soldiers are trying to make their way past the Indian Army, taking cover in the darkness and the dense vegetation. At the crack of dawn, Indian Air Force Hunters appear in the sky and strafe the area, taking on the convoy of Pakistani vehicles and soldiers who are trying to run away. They cause utter devastation among the enemy forces and also send back a tactical report informing the ground forces that they have spotted small enemy columns trying to bypass the battalion-defended area.

The next morning, Lali is told to take a patrol of ten soldiers and ambush escaping enemy columns. MMG platoon commander, Capt. Surjit Singh, who goes to check on the young officer soon after orders have been passed, finds him meticulously planning the ambush in textbook style and loses his temper. 'What the hell are you still doing here?' he bellows. 'Get out of here and get on with the task.' A jittery Lali immediately sets out.

The patrol makes its way across the swampy, marshy river terrain. Suddenly, there is a gunshot. Paratrooper Janardan Nair, one of the two scouts, has been shot in the arm. Lali spots two men in khaki running away into the shrubbery. They disappear into the foliage. A bleeding Nair is told to walk back and seek medical help while the rest of the patrol takes position inside the foliage. The shrubbery is so dense that even Lali, who stands taller than six feet, cannot be spotted behind it. Soon, the men hear the sound of heavy boots—enemy soldiers are in sight. Lali steps forward and, lifting his Sten gun, fires at them. His men follow suit. Since each paratrooper has only one magazine, in thirty seconds their ammunition is finished. They fall back into the foliage. When they do a body count, they find one man missing. The missing paratrooper is identified as Lance Havildar Joseph Martha, who has been handling the light machine gun.

All of a sudden, artillery shells start dropping from the sky. Lali finds Captain Surjit coming in his direction along with two soldiers. Surjit informs him that they are getting artillery support and tells him to extricate and return to the unit. Lali does not want to go back without his missing comrade but Surjit orders him to do so, reassuring him that he will send a team to the site of the ambush. When the team returns, it finds Martha dead. He has taken a burst in the left temple. His body is brought back by his fellow soldiers with heavy hearts.

~

At 1600 hours, 2 PARA spots a massive column of troops advancing in their direction—the Indian Army's 95 Infantry Brigade is moving towards Dacca after vanquishing the enemy. The leading columns are of 1 Maratha. With textbook precision, the airborne forces and ground forces have linked up within the stipulated twenty-four hours. Since 2 PARA is the old 3 Maratha, there is an emotional Maratha reunion near Poongli Bridge. Then, 1 Maratha crosses the 2 PARA location, marches across Poongli Bridge and goes into Tangail. It is followed by 167 Brigade, also returning after action on the Jamalpur side.

At 0900 hours on 12 December, information is received that Tangail has been vacated by the enemy forces. A force is sent to Tangail to occupy it. On the evening of 12 December, the battle at Tangail is over. Peace reigns at Poongli Bridge. The same evening, Lali is called to the battalion command. He goes nervously, wondering if he is going to get ticked off for something he did wrong. All the officers stand seriously as he enters, making him sweat even in the cold. Col Pannu glares at him and then steps forward with a smile to pin a Para Wing on his shirtsleeve. He also gets an extra star and is promoted to the field rank of captain. The twenty-one-year-old's dream has come true.

Victory

2 PARA goes on to march into Dacca with the other Indian forces. They engage and dislodge the enemy from Mirpur Bridge, on the outskirts of Dacca, on the night of 15–16 November, and on 16 December at 1100 hours, they are the first unit to enter Dacca. The paratroopers watch the public surrender ceremony, standing right behind the photographers taking that iconic picture of Gen. J.S. Aurora and Gen. A.A.K. Niazi signing the document of surrender. They watch as Gen. Niazi is taken into custody, his belt and weapon removed. They observe the scramble for souvenirs as people take his epaulets, his car flag, the star plates on the car, and the pen used to sign the surrender document. The battalion is now assigned the job of providing a safe and secure corridor to the Pakistan Army, keeping at bay the Mukti Bahini that is out in full strength seeking revenge.

On 17 December, the unit moves back to Tangail, from where they are brought back to Guwahati by army transport, and from there to the New Bogaigaon train station. A special train brings them back to Delhi Cantonment where they have been told to participate in the Republic Day parade. The train reaches Delhi Cantonment on the evening of 31 December, and the soldiers spill out in high spirits. 'We got into our jeeps in our dirty, ripped fatigues and had a field run that night,' remembers Col Gill, his face lit up by a smile of remembrance. 'We drove down to the Dhaula Kuan Club, then to the Oberoi hotel, which had a disco called the Tabela. No one charged us anything that night; we were treated like heroes. From there we went to Connaught Place and drove around the Inner Circle and the Outer Circle in our jeeps fitted with RCL guns. No one was celebrating the New Year; they were all celebrating the war victory.'

The soldiers are greeted with marigold garlands and loud whoops of joy; proud citizens lift them on their shoulders; crowds are out on the roads with the tricolour in their hands and cheerfully waving kids on their shoulders. Wherever they go, the soldiers are greeted with open arms and wide smiles. They are treated like heroes. Bangladesh has been born.

Author's Note

In February 1972, 2nd Lt (later Col) Lali Gill went on to do his Para Basic Course from the Paratrooper Training School in Agra and the mandatory training jumps that officially entitled him to jump from an air force aircraft. He finally formally acquired his well-deserved Para Wings. He is possibly the only paratrooper in world military history who jumped straight into the battlefield without any training or wings. The proud colonel is now seventy-one years old and settled in Mohali.

A Strange Gift

8 December 1971
The Great Indian Desert
Pakistan

10 Sikh Light Infantry has crossed the Indian border in Rajasthan and gone 45 km in, where it has made contact with the Pakistan Army. The Battle of Parbat Ali rages in the bitter cold—the proud Sikh warriors have burrowed into trenches dug in the sand and are facing not just enemy infantry but also air strikes. Far in the distance, a lone Indian Army jeep is making its way through the golden-yellow sand dunes. It is headed in the direction of the gunfire. A young Army Medical Corps doctor in uniform—dark-skinned, slim and tall—is seated in front. He raises his hand sharply. His driver, a hefty Sikh soldier with a dense beard and moustache, steps down hard on the brakes, making the jeep skid. It screeches to a stop, throwing a fountain of sand into the air.

Enemy MMG fire is on them now. Twenty-five-year-old Capt. Dr David Muthumani, the newly posted regimental medical officer of the unit, has never been in battle before and is feeling a little out of place. The bullets come so fast that he cannot see them but they are zipping over his head and perforating the dunes, creating fissures that quickly get filled up with slithering sand. '*Cover lo. Jaldi*!' he shouts, turning to face his two Sikh nursing assistants sitting in the back seat. All of them, including the driver, jump out of the vehicle and crawl under it. The medical team has been told to stay out of the range of enemy fire and wait for injured soldiers to be brought to them, but David knows that if he waits it might be too late for some. He has told himself he will not let a single man die if he can help it, and he intends to keep that promise.

'*Main crawl kar ke aage jata hun, mere pichhe aao*,' he tells his team. Then, with his helmet strapped tight and knapsack stacked with emergency medicines, morphine injections, bandages and tourniquets, David crawls out from under the vehicle and starts pulling himself forward, keeping his head close to the ground, trying to ignore the frightening screams of shells above his head.

Two Months Ago

10 Sikh LI had been in Bombay when it received orders to move to Munabao in the Barmer district of Rajasthan—the last village on the Indo–Pak border. War clouds were looming and it was expected that the battalion would soon be sent on an attack. On the night of 3 December, soon after the battalion had beaten 2 Mahar in an inter-battalion

football match, war was declared against Pakistan. The unit was tasked to cross the border. All the football players quickly changed into their fatigues, laced up their boots, strapped on their helmets and, with ammunition and rations in their backpacks, marched into Pakistan, most of them limping from the strain of the match. The medical team of around twenty personnel, led by Capt. David, was asked to follow two hours later in a one-ton (army truck).

The Pakistanis had already blown up the Munabao–Khokrapar (India–Pakistan) railway track, fearing the Indian Army would use it to cart ammunition and food supplies. The Indian soldiers had to walk all night and take sleep breaks during the daytime, either resting inside or under their vehicles, making sure to camouflage these with gunny sacks and sand since the Pakistan Air Force had started strafing the area.

Early on the morning of 8 December, David received a message on the radio set. '*Ladai chid gayi hai, daktar sahab. Hamari casualties hui hain. CO sahab ka aadesh hai aap march kar den,*' the soldier manning the set at the other end had said. A frantic David had asked his team to quickly pack up. He knew that for the injured, bleeding soldiers, every second counted. Without losing any time, the medical team had got on to their one-ton and driven across the desert as fast as they could. They had soon run into Lt Col Basant Singh, the cool and composed commanding officer of the unit, a proud Sikh himself, who was monitoring the battle. Finding the medical team negotiating its way across the desert in the slow, lumbering truck, he had offered

David his own jeep. Being lighter, it would travel faster and also be less noticeable to the Pakistan Air Force. The heavy vehicle was quickly camouflaged with gunny bags and sand while the doctor and his team drove off in the CO's jeep.

On the Battlefield

Spreadeagled in the sand, David is trying to move as fast as he can. His nursing assistants follow, their rifles dragging behind them, making snaking trails in the golden sand. Following the direction where the bullets are coming from, they soon reach the spot where the unit is fighting from the trenches. MMGs boom, shells are screaming overhead, men are shouting in violent rage, and those who have been hit are crying out in pain. The team crawls around, listening for the laboured breathing of those who have been shot or have had limbs torn away by grenade blasts. Charlie Company commander Major Sharma has been shot through his pelvis and is among the injured. Unmindful of the danger to their own lives, David and his boys start administering first aid. They inject painkillers into slashed limbs, tie tourniquets around bleeding thighs, apply antiseptic on gaping cuts. Then, one by one, they start dragging the wounded to where the jeep waits, keeping their own heads down, hoping that even if they are hit, the bullets will bounce off their helmets.

~

24 December 1971
1030 hours

A week has passed since ceasefire was declared. The young doctor has lost a lot of weight. His uniform falls loosely on his slim frame. His face and hands are scarred and badly sunburnt. His moustache is now bushy, his hair untidily overgrown, his uniform stained with blood and gunfire. He has only two sets, and there is no water to wash, so he wears one and airs out the other, interchanging them every two days. Today, he is driving across the desert. Warm rays of the morning sun fall on the vast, endless ocean of sand, turning it the colour of molten gold. There are only dunes as far as the eye can see. Shimmering, shifting, changing place in the wind—mute witnesses to the war yet unscarred by it.

Though shattered vehicles and burnt shells still lie buried in the sand, the battle-weary soldiers have finally found peace. The Indian Army is still inside Pakistan, not having received orders to move back. The troops live in bunkers dug in the sand and tents pitched between the dunes. Comrades lost have been cremated in the battlefield, serious casualties have been shifted to military hospitals across the border. David, who has been moved around from one place to another depending upon where he was needed most during the war, is now in charge of the advance dressing station (ADS) of 31 Brigade, also located in the desert.

Just this morning, David was surprised to find the radio operator looking for him with news that the CO of a nearby unit wanted to talk to him. He had rushed to the radio set to find Lt Col Basant Singh on the line. 'Happy Christmas, oye, David. *Kaisa hai tu*?' he had boomed over the wireless, informing David that the unit was located just a few kilometres away. 'Come and have Christmas lunch with us,' he had said, and a delighted David had immediately agreed.

Since the war has ended, other than the occasional snakebite or cases of dehydration, David has no serious patients to look after. Most of his time is now spent staring into the horizon, wondering when the army will get orders to move back to India. Or lying in his bunker thinking of home in Tirupati. His bunker, which he has dug himself, is a seven-foot-deep pit lined on the sides with corrugated galvanized iron (CGI) sheets to prevent sand from caving in. The roof is made of metal sheets and rods scavenged from vehicles destroyed during the war, on top of which is a two-foot layer of sand, which keeps his bunker five degrees warmer in the winter. The warmth is inviting for other creatures too.

David remembers the day he woke up to alarmed cries of '*saanp, saanp*'. Still groggy from sleep, he looked up to find his buddy peering inside the tent. '*Kahan hai saanp*?' David asked. The reply froze his blood. '*Sahab, aapke upar*.' He looked down to find a snake coiled on top of his blanket. Paralysed with fear since he knew that the place was rampant with poisonous vipers, he soon gathered his wits and asked the soldier to move out of the way. Then, with a quick flick of his wrists, he threw the blanket off and leaped out of the snake's way.

Now, of course, he is in his jeep, a frayed map of the area on the seat next to him, driving down to meet the unit he had served in war. He regrets that he can't be better dressed. Since the retreating Pakistan Army destroyed the Munabao–Khokrapar railway track, water and rations are brought by road from Barmer and are strictly rationed. Since early December, all soldiers have been subsisting on 5 litres of water per day, which they use for drinking, washing and bodily functions. Washing clothes is completely out of the question. No one has had a bath since the beginning of December. David has managed to shave and wash his face with soap, a luxury he reserves for himself once in two days. He hopes he's not smelling too much.

He is looking forward to seeing his old comrades—the brave and boisterous Sikh troops with whom he has trekked through the desert and broken bread in the langar, whose Punjabi jokes he hasn't always understood but still smiled at, whose hands he has held in pain, whose wounds he has dressed, who have shared his sorrow, standing moist-eyed as he bid farewell to those that his hands could not heal and whose eyes he had to shut one last time gently with his palm.

David remembers the month of October, when he met them for the first time, soon after he was posted to 10 Sikh LI. The troops had accepted him as one of their own, in spite of his broken command over Hindi and no knowledge of Punjabi. To David, who had been sent as the RMO, they soon become comrades he had to bring back alive from the battlefield. To them, he became their 'Isai daktar sahab' who would stand by them in the face of death.

A special train had taken the feisty Sikh troops from Mumbai to Munabao, where they had camped among the sand dunes. War clouds were looming but till orders came for attack, the men had little to do besides physical training (PT) parades and eating three times a day in the mess established at the location. Often, the officers would get the troops around a sand model and brief them on what was to be the course of action when/if war broke out. The Sikh troops were typically full of josh and an '*aan do, dekh laange*' spirit. So much so that one day in the CO's darbar, Rifleman Jaswant Singh, not older than twenty, had stood up holding a letter from home, his eyes flashing. His mother had asked him to die for the country, he had said. '*Assi taiyaar haan*,' he had stated proudly, bringing a wide smile to Col Basant's face. Later, he had indeed lost his life during the Battle of Parbat Ali. David wondered how proud his mother would be of him, and how heartbroken.

David also remembers how once, when marching for battle, subsisting on limited rations, they had come upon an abandoned truck that was carrying boiled eggs to troops in the forward area. Possibly abandoned after being strafed by enemy aircraft, it stood deserted. The boys had climbed in and feasted on the most delicious boiled eggs they had ever had in their lives, and then, satiated, fallen into a deep slumber.

He also remembers another experience that had upset him in battle but that he now dismisses with a shrug. His memory takes him to his first day at the 85 Brigade Advance Dressing Station that was established to attend to casualties from all units in battle. David had driven without a break from the 10 Sikh LI war location and reached there to find approximately thirty soldiers lying seriously injured and dehydrated, moaning for water and pain relief. He moved from one man to another, assessing their condition, prioritizing those who needed immediate attention. Mostly mine blast victims, they had had their limbs blown off and needed pain relief, resuscitation and haemorrhage control. For the young doctor, looking at such injuries was a big initial shock by itself, but he soon got used to it. The treatment fell into a pattern. Give painkiller, stem bleeding and then move the injured to the Field Hospital at Munabao in waiting ambulances. He had no time to even think or pause for a cup of tea till late at night. After all the injured had been attended to, David just fell upon the sand and went to sleep.

The next morning, around 0400 hours, more casualties started coming in. The ADS also got a visit from the new brigade commander who had just got posted there. He saw wounded soldiers lying in the open, crying out in pain. When he asked for the doctor on duty, he was taken to David, who was sitting on the ground with a soldier's leg in his lap, trying to apply a tourniquet to his thigh to stem the bleeding. Part of the soldier's leg had been blown up by a mine. David's uniform was filthy and his face stained with grime and blood. The brigade commander was furious at the doctor's stubble and shabby physical appearance. He started shouting at David, who did not even look up since he was so busy tending to his patient. Finally, running out of patience, he turned around and asked politely, 'Sir, would you rather I go and shave or will you let me attend to the injured soldiers?' The shamed brigade commander walked away.

~

Laughing out loud at that memory, David checks the map again. The battalion should be around here somewhere, he tell himself. He peers into the horizon. Far in the distance between the golden dunes, he can spot some signs of habitation. He steps on the accelerator and drives on, sand crunching under his jeep's tyres, the cold wind making his eyes water.

All of a sudden, his eyes catch sight of men in faded uniforms and olive-green patkas, and the sound of loud cheering reaches his ears. Tall, hefty, smiling Sikh soldiers stand at attention as his jeep drives in. He is surprised to find that the entire regiment of more than 700 men is lined up to receive him. Company commanders, subedar major, JCOs, troops—they all wait on both sides, grinning widely at him. David quickly parks his jeep and jumps out, fixing his beret. He walks up to Col Basant and salutes him smartly.

Basant has an affectionate smile on his battle-hardened face. 'Happy Christmas, *mere babbar sher*,' he says. '*Haddi ho gaya hai tu. Theek se khana nahi khila rahe tujhe brigade mein?'* Stepping forward to hold David in a warm embrace, he turns to the men. '*Aa gaya tumhara Isai daktar sahab*,' he says. The soldiers have started cheering. '*Daktar sahab ki jai ho*!' they call out, making David's cheeks burn with embarrassment.

'*Khana-shana hota rahega, David. Uske pehle tere liye ek gift hai unit ki taraf se*,' Col Basant says, patting the young doctor affectionately on his back. The entire unit walks the puzzled doctor down to where stands a big steel bucket of water with a mug and a towel placed alongside. 'Every soldier has contributed one glass of water for you,' Col Basant tells him. 'Take a bath. This is a Christmas gift from 10 Sikh LI for their favourite daktar sahab who bravely faced bullets with us.'

As the amused troops watch, a terribly self-conscious David takes off his boots and socks and then steps out of his trousers and shirt. To the sound of loud clapping, he dips his fingers into the clean, warm water. '*Magga utha lo, sahab*,' the unit subedar major calls out. The soldiers laugh. Taking the white enamel mug, David dips it into the bucket and pours water over his head. It trickles down his face and torso in what feels like a warm embrace after the stressful days of battle. He bends down to repeat the process. Closing his eyes, he slowly pours water over his head again, and again. He does it till the water is nearly finished and then he lifts up the bucket using both hands and tilts it over his head, letting the last drops trickle on to his face. And then he quickly reaches for the towel to wipe his face. He does not want his comrades to see his flowing tears.

Author's Note

In October 1971, Capt. Dr David Muthumani was posted as RMO to 10 Sikh LI. He was with the brave Sikhs in the Battle of Parbat Ali.

This story is based on interviews with Col Basant Singh (retd), who commanded 10 Sikh LI during the war, and Capt. Dr David Muthumani (retd). Col Basant is now eighty-eight years old and lives in Meerut. Capt. David is seventy-five and settled in Tirupati. He has lost sight in one eye because of glaucoma but is otherwise perfectly fit. He left the army soon after the war to join a mission hospital. He says that the desert bath was the best gift he has ever received in his life.

Behind Enemy Lines

November 1971
Plassey, Nadia district
West Bengal

Dusk has fallen. Chiman Singh's luminescent brown eyes are fixed on the young Bangla boys he and his comrades have trained. He has taught them all that he could in the short span of time he was given—diving, handling bombs, scraping seaweed and moss off the hulls of parked ships with bare hands, attaching limpet mines to them and then blowing them up sky-high. Now, it is time for his trainees to cross the border into East Pakistan and put his lessons into practice.

Most of the boys are in their early twenties. Nearly all of them have told him heartbreaking tales of poverty, humiliation and abuse. Chiman remembers the day they came to him. Thirsty and starving, having escaped their own land to save their lives, stomachs curved in and sticking to their ribs. He remembers how they had started eating half-cooked rice with bare hands, like starving animals, scooping it up in their palms and pushing it into their mouths, not waiting for dal or vegetables. His heart bleeds for the pain they have been subjected to. Chiman himself has a seething fury inside him at the perpetrators of evil.

'*Saar, aapniyo cholen na aamader saathe* (Sir, please come with us),' Nazrul Islam is pleading. He is a defector from the Pakistan Navy who has joined the movement for a free Bangladesh. But Chiman is not allowed to cross the border. The Indian government has steadfastly been claiming it is only providing humanitarian aid to the refugees. Fifteen pairs of young, scared eyes are looking at him with trepidation. '*Saar, aapni saathe thaakle aamago himmat baadbe, aar kaaj o bhalobhabe saarbe* (If you come with us, we will be more confident. And the mission shall also get done),' Nazrul is saying. Chiman has a young wife and frail old parents in Gokulgarh village, Haryana. If he is caught, he will be killed. If he survives, he risks humiliation, court martial, dismissal from service or imprisonment. His wife won't even get his pension. But at that moment, he doesn't care.

Taking off his Omega diver's watch and his identity card and removing all the Indian currency he has on him, Chiman walks across to the civil truck that has ferried the boys and places his belongings inside. Stepping out of his shoes and shirt, he cuts off the 'Made in India' labels with his penknife. Once satisfied that he is carrying no signs of his Indian identity, Chiman looks at the anxiously waiting boys. '*Chalbo*!' he says, a smile cutting across his handsome face. The young faces light up even in the darkness. Folding up their lungis for better mobility, the boys start walking with a new spring in their step. In twos and threes, they disappear into the dense vegetation. Chiman follows silently, his 9 mm sterling machine gun (SMG) slung across his lithe, muscular back. Without a glance back at the country he is leaving behind, he crosses into East Pakistan. It is time to settle scores!

The Beginning

April 1971
Cochin

In March 1971, soon after Sheikh Mujibur Rahman declares an independent government in East Pakistan after the Awami League wins the elections with a huge majority, Gen. Tikka Khan orders the Pakistan Army to take control. On the night of 25 March 1971, Mujib is arrested and flown to West Pakistan, and a ghastly genocide is launched to subjugate the Bengali people who are revolting for their own country—Bangladesh. Frightened refugees cross the border and start infiltrating into India in massive numbers to save their lives.

Infuriated by stories of the rape and killing of their own people, Bengali officers in the Pakistani defence forces start defecting. Around this time, eight Bengali sailors undergoing training in France to acquire a new submarine have deserted and asked for asylum in India. Naval chief Admiral S.M. Nanda is asked if they can be made use of in conflict. He entrusts the task to Lt Samir Das, diving instructor at the diving school in Cochin, who in turn selects his team of eight people for the mission. The team includes clearance divers Lt Kapil V.P. and Chief Seaman Chiman Singh, specialists in deploying as well as clearing underwater mines. They are sent to INS *Hoogly* (rechristened INS *Netaji Subhash* in 1974) in Calcutta.

In Calcutta, the team is told that it shall be training young Bengali boys to be naval guerrillas, and a training ground needs to be identified for this purpose. A suitable stretch of land is found in Plassey, on the banks of the Bhagirathi River. 'The water was 8–10 feet and there were no crocodiles in the river which made it perfect for training. We cleared the sugar cane fields on the banks of the river and a ground was made ready,' says Chiman. The naval team is put up in the Plassey Circuit House with 2nd Sikh LI (Light Infantry) providing logistical support.

The team members start visiting refugee camps, meeting camp commandants and scouting for young, fit boys around twenty years of age who are good swimmers and have the fire within to take on the establishment. Nearly 300 are recruited. 'We brought the selected boys to our camp at Plassey,' Chiman remembers. 'Almost everyone was passionate about joining us. They had walked miles, been assaulted by the Razakars and helplessly watched women being raped, cash being looted and cows being driven away. They were seething with rage. Lt Das told us that the boys had to be trained to destabilize ships, blow up jetties, cut off anchors of ships; in general, to cause complete chaos. We had been trained to do the same.'

The Training

The boys are woken up before daybreak, taken for a run and made to do some rigorous physical training. After breakfast, they attend sessions where they are taught to identify and handle explosives, fix limpet mines and fit plastic explosive charges on the hulls of ships. 'We showed them how to take limpet mines into the water in buddy pairs, with one man guiding the other who had the mine strapped to his chest. We showed them how to cut anchors of ships, handle highly explosive TNT, how to time explosions so they could get away before the blast took place, etc.,' says Chiman.

It is essential to not have the Indian Navy (or government) linked to the training in any way. Identities of the Indian Navy staff acting as trainers are not disclosed to anyone. Everyone is addressed as 'sir'. 'None of us addressed each other by name; we wore no uniforms; everyone was dressed in shorts and swimming trunks; we used Hindi, English and some Bangla to communicate with them,' Chiman explains. In three months the training is complete. The commandos are now ready for action. As 14 August—Pakistan's Independence Day—draws close, a daring plan is hatched.

A Musical Interlude

14 August 1971
0600 hours

Nobody notices small groups of about a dozen men, dressed in faded cotton lungis and chappals, quietly collecting in secure houses (belonging to Mukti Bahini supporters) near riverbanks all along East Pakistan. Narayanganj, Chandpur, Chalna and Mongla are some of the locations where they have reached, carrying in their backpacks and *jholas* explosives, mines, limpets, etc. They have been launched from different places, and the move has been timed in such a way that they all reach their respective destinations a day before 14 August. What is common between all teams are the identical radio sets that they are all listening to.

All of a sudden, all ears perk up. Pankaj Mullick's sonorous voice permeates into the air. All India Radio (AIR) is playing his beautiful Bangla number '*Aami tomai joto, shuniye chchilem gaan; taar bodole aami, chaa i ne kono daan*'. Written by Rabindranath Tagore, it means, 'For all the songs I have sung to you, I seek nothing in return.' The lyrics, however, imply much more than that. The song is a signal to all the naval commandos waiting at different locations that the planned attacks shall go ahead as decided. The boys look at each other in nervous excitement. The time has come to avenge the deaths of their people. 'This is a suicide squad; only those willing to sacrifice their lives for the cause should enrol,' the words of their prime minister in exile, Tajuddin Ahmed, ring out in their ears.

Around midnight, the commandos kick off their plastic slippers and strip off their lungis. They wade into the water in their underwear, wincing as the cold water lashes their skinny bodies. With limpet mines strapped to their chests, they swim across to pre-identified ships, jetties and boats. That night, the water explodes around East Pakistan. The next morning, the entire world wakes up to this powerful expression of fury from the local people against the demonic regime of Tikka Khan.

'The song signals through AIR were done right under the nose of the enemy yet were understood only by those for whom they were meant,' Chiman recounts. 'A Bengali officer had been deputed with AIR. He had sat in their workstation and asked for particular songs to be played, saying they were meant to cheer up soldiers in the forces. Completely ignorant about the real reasons behind the request, AIR had obliged,' says Chiman.

The simultaneously coordinated sea attacks come as a nasty shock to the Pakistani government. An astounding twenty-five vessels are hit in an hour's time. These include merchant ships, steamers, pontoons and cargo barges. Ships drift into the sea, many sink and some block waterways, crippling the administration completely. Chiman and the other trainers hear the news with great satisfaction. Submariner Miandad is the only one who does not report back—his body is never found—but all the other boys return to the camp. 'No proof could be found to link the attack to India, though people had started suspecting it,' Chiman explains.

Chiman is sent to Agartala to handle another camp but is recalled in October. A second attack is being planned. He is again interacting with his 'bacche'. This time, he is responsible for launching them across the border through a land route.

~

When the nervous boys implore him to come with them, Chiman cannot say no. Having left behind all identifying marks of his Indianness, he slings his SMG across his back and crosses the border with them.

For ten days, the motley group moves through coconut groves and villages, never stopping in one place for more than a night. Chiman is living with a constant throbbing fear that he will be discovered and killed. The Mukti Bahini guides have identified safe houses at each stop, usually belonging to Awami League supporters who give them place to sleep, food to eat and access to the all-purpose small ponds in most courtyards used for keeping fish, washing utensils, bathing, etc. In return they get Pakistani currency and a certificate that says they have been helpful. Chiman is so paranoid about getting caught that he keeps his loaded rifle at arm's length even when he is taking a dip in a pond. He is mentally prepared to push the barrel in his mouth and shoot himself if he feels arrest cannot be avoided.

A Trail of Destruction

The group walks across East Pakistan for ten days, covering more than 20 km each night, sleeping through the day and venturing out after dusk, constantly on the lookout for targets to destroy. They blow up a pontoon boat getting rations for troops, a jetty, transmitters, high-tension wires and whatever else they can find. With Chiman overseeing operations, they do their work flawlessly in the darkness of the night, slipping away quietly into the dense vegetation just as the explosions take place, without leaving any clues behind. 'We had thought these actions would destabilize the government in a few years' time. We never imagined Bangladesh would be formed so soon,' Chiman remarks. '*Ye Pakistani toh bahut hi darpok nikle. Inhone kuch dum hi nahi dikhaya. Itne jaldi haar maan gaye.*'

Chiman lives under the constant, constricting fear of being found out. 'Being tall and well-built, I would stand out among the small and thin boys in the team. People could immediately guess that I was not a Bengali.' Though he has learnt the kalima and all the rituals associated with reading the namaz so that he can pass for a Muslim, Chiman refuses to eat beef since he is a Hindu. In one village, when he is offered the meat of a calf that has been slaughtered in front of his eyes, he pretends to have an upset stomach and does not eat.

He remembers another incident. 'In one of the shelters, I met an old lady who told me, "*Aami jano tumi Hindu aashe.*"' Her entire family has gone to Calcutta, leaving her behind because she is too weak and old to walk. She pleads with Chiman to take her along and unite her with her family. Chiman says he did not return by the same route. 'I have no idea *us maa ke saath kya hua.* I regret that I could not help her.'

Finally, the team reaches Barisal, East Pakistan's second largest riverine post built on the banks of the Kirtankhola River. From there they decide to return to Plassey where, unbeknown to them, a massive hunt has been going on for Chiman, or 'C. Singh', as he is popularly called.

Back Where He Belongs

22 November 1971
Boyra

Clad in faded lungis, rifles slung across their backs, Chiman and Nazrul Islam are walking back towards India along with their group of commandos. They have no idea that the Indian Army has entered East Pakistan. At Boyra, the group walks into the battle location of 22 Rajput just when a dogfight starts in the sky. Hearing the air-raid siren, Chiman and his boys jump into the trenches. They are subjected to a volley of Haryanvi abuse from the troops and rudely thrown out. 'We had no option but to stand in the open while the planes fought overhead. I did not tell them that I am also from Haryana,' Chiman says with a laugh. Two of the Sabres are knocked down and some of the soldiers go in search of the ejected pilots, who can be seen dropping down on parachutes.

Chiman is presented before the unit's CO, who finds it hard to believe that the bearded, lungi-clad, Haryanvi-speaking man who carries no proof of identity is from the Indian Navy. Chiman is taken to Fort William, where he is interviewed by Maj. Gen. J.F.R. Jacob, chief of staff of the Indian Army's Eastern Command, and a signal saying 'C. Singh is back' is sent to his CO in Plassey. Chiman is detained for intelligence clearance. He is suspected to be a spy. No one can believe that he went underground out of empathy with the Bangla people and walked more than 200 km, risking his life, reputation and pension for the cause. 'They interrogated me for so many days that I finally lost my patience and told the captain sahab questioning me, "Either you set me free or shoot me, but I will not suffer this humiliation any more,"' Chiman remembers.

Chiman finally gets intelligence clearance. On 3 December, war is declared and his old comrade Lt Kapil V.P. turns up at Fort William to take him back. On 8 December, Chiman and Kapil accompany Commander Samant to Hasnabad, from where Samant has planned a gunboat raid that will strike the Khulna–Mongla industrial complex and further destabilize the Pakistan Army. The fleet, named Force Alpha, includes the gunboats *Padma* and *Palash*, and the naval ship *Panvel*. While Kapil is taken aboard the *Palash*, Chiman boards the *Padma*. He is going right back into East Pakistan.

~

10 December 1971
1140 hours
On board gunboat *Padma*
Rupsha River
Khulna, East Pakistan

The air is cold but the lukewarm sun feels good on his back. Leading seaman Chiman is lying prone on the deck. A light machine gun is nestled in his arms. He is watching the buildings lining the shore with narrowed eyes. He can make out sandbags stacked on the roofs and knows there are armed enemy soldiers behind them with loaded rifles in their hands. Their aim is to blow up the Khulna naval base and pressurize Pakistani troops, who are already under attack from land, by attacking them from the riverside also.

Two duck boats—both about 100 feet long—have been refitted with two 40/60 mm Bofors guns each for the covert operation. Laden with explosives, they carry Mukti Bahini boys who have been trained as assault swimmers. MV (motor vehicle) *Palash*, commanded by Lt Cdr Jayanto Kumar Roy Choudhury, is leading. MV *Padma*, commanded by Lt Suvesh Kumar Mitter, is right behind it. The Indian naval ship *Panvel*, commanded by Lt Cdr J.P.A. Noronha, is following the two gunboats. It has on board the man behind Force Alfa: Cdr M.N.R. Samant. While the *Panvel* crew is dressed in khaki navy rig, the two gunboats look like they are headed for a cruise, with most people in colourful T-shirts and shorts.

Each boat has on board one Border Security Force soldier armed with an LMG.

Gnats in the Air

Feeling sympathetic towards BSF constable Chintal Sharma, the boat's lone armed escort, Chiman asks him to take a cigarette and chai break, offering to man his position in the meantime. The grateful soldier takes up the offer, returning dutifully in fifteen minutes. He sprawls next to Chiman and takes the LMG back from him.

Suddenly, there is the deep-throated roar of fighter planes in the sky, and they both look up to find three Gnats flying towards them. 'Since the PAF did not have any air presence in East Pakistan, we didn't worry much, knowing these had to be our own fighters,' says Chiman, talking to me in his airy, sunlit home in Rewari, Haryana. 'We had also stretched out bright yellow awnings on the bridge, which was an agreed-upon air signal that these were friendly boats,' he says. However, much to the horror of the boat crew, the planes mistake them for Pakistani vessels and swoop down for an attack.

Two rockets fall on the *Padma*. The air rings out with the scream of men in pain, and Chiman watches in disbelief as the boat catches fire in front of his eyes. 'The second rocket grazed my thigh and smashed into the BSF soldier by my side,' he recounts. 'He blew up into smithereens in front of my eyes. When I looked at myself, the flesh on my leg had just melted and I could see bones sticking out of my thigh.' The rocket goes through the bridge where the captain of the boat, Lt Mitter, his quartermaster Mohmmad Abdul Haque (a defected Pakistan Navy sailor) and squadron engineer officer Lt J.V. Natu are standing. It takes a chunk of flesh off Mitter's right arm, splits open Natu's stomach and slices off Haque's right leg.

A profusely bleeding Chiman watches helplessly as the planes return and bomb the *Palash*. He hears Mitter calling out 'abandon ship' in English and then in Bangla. Despite being in excruciating pain, Chiman drags himself to the edge of the boat and drops into the water along with the others jumping in to save their lives. The fighter planes return and, flying low over the river, start targeting the survivors. 'Each time I saw a plane coming, I would hold my breath and go underwater,' says Chiman. Meanwhile, sympathetic detonations have started on the explosives-laden gunboats. The mines start going off one after another. The two boats are on fire.

Survivors who manage to swim to the shore find armed enemy soldiers waiting for them. Many are shot dead in the shallow water. Those fit to run make a dash for freedom. Chiman can barely reach the beach. He lies in the wet sand, covered in clay, half his body still in water. The Pakistani soldiers call out for him to surrender. When he does not respond, they shoot him in the back. 'I tried to get up but my legs just collapsed under me. I could not even lift my head. I lay there bleeding in the water, waiting to die,' he remembers.

A Brush with Death

Once satisfied that he is unarmed, the Pakistani soldiers walk up to Chiman, who is lying lifeless in the sand. The sergeant is fascinated by the Omega diver's watch on his wrist. '*Aisa ghadi toh pehle kabhi dekha nahin*,' he is saying.

'They wanted my watch but were afraid that it might be wired for explosives. I told them to take it, assuring them that it would not explode.'

Another soldier spots Chiman's gold wedding ring that is now stuck on his swollen finger. He comes forward with his bayonet, intending to cut the finger off. 'Just pull it off, don't cut my finger,' Chiman whispers hoarsely. The man kneels down and forces the ring off, stripping the flesh from Chiman's bloated finger along with it. The soldiers start dragging Chiman across the road but the sudden scream of air-raid sirens makes them drop him and run for shelter. Chiman passes out with the pain and blood loss.

Prisoner of War

11 December 1971
Khulna

Slipping between a blood-loss-induced coma and consciousness, Chiman wakes up in a dark and dingy room. He is alert enough to realize that Mitter and Natu, both seriously injured, are in the same room. All three have been made POWs by the Pakistanis.

Their wounds have been tended to by surgeons. The bullets lodged in Chiman's back have been extracted; shrapnel has been taken out of Natu's stomach and it has been stitched up; Mitter's arm has been operated upon multiple times. All three are heavily bandaged and in unbearable pain. The prisoners are offered some dal and roti but they are in no state to eat. For a week, the three lie unattended, hearing air-raid sirens, planes passing overhead and sounds of battle. 'We would pray for a bomb to drop on us so that our misery might end,' Chiman remembers.

Panacea

On 16 December, the door of their room opens and sunlight streams in, blinding them with its intensity. They see flashes of olive green and cannot believe their eyes. The Indian Army has found them. 'The soldiers walked in and offered us some chocolates to eat. I was so relieved that I started crying,' Chiman remembers. They later find out that Haque was picked up by the *Panvel* but could not survive. Chiman, Mitter and Natu are taken to a nearby airstrip from where a Dakota aircraft brings them to the Base Hospital at Barrackpore.

All three are given enemas since they haven't relived themselves for a week. The hospital is overflowing with war casualties. Local women volunteers give the patients baths, shave them and comb their matted hair. Chiman's wound is so badly infected that he cries out in pain each time it is dressed, begging nurses not to touch it. The wound has gone untreated for so long that it has acquired septicaemia.

Chiman is initially shifted to the Secunderabad Military Hospital and then to the Indian Naval Hospital Ship (INHS) *Asvini* in Colaba, Mumbai, where he receives a visit from Prime Minister Indira Gandhi. His Maha Vir Chakra has also been announced. 'I was on the beach sitting on some rocks when I was hastily summoned and asked to lie down on the bed. Mrs Gandhi was coming to see me,' Chiman smiles, remembering the day he had a conversation with a cheerful, indulgent Mrs Gandhi.

On 31 March 1972, Chiman starts walking on crutches and is sent to Delhi for the investiture ceremony. He asks for ten days' leave and goes home to his village near Delhi and meets his wife, proudly bringing to her his sparkling Maha Vir Chakra, pinned on his shirt by President V.V. Giri. He reports back to INHS *Asvini* and, once deemed fit, is transferred to the diving school at Cochin. His wound has taken nearly six months to heal. The only sailor to be decorated with the Maha Vir Chakra leaves the navy in 1972 after completing ten years of service.

Author's Note

This story is based on an interview with Petty Officer Chiman Singh, Maha Vir Chakra.

Chiman left the navy in 1972 and went to the Gulf to work as a commercial diver, drawing the same monthly salary then as the President of India, a princely Rs 10,000. In 1982, he decided to quit and returned to Gokalgarh village in Haryana to be with his wife and two daughters.

Looking back at the covert operation where he nearly lost his life, Chiman says, 'I survived. But I have no idea what happened to the boys we had trained. They had no names, no numbers. Those who could must have escaped; those who couldn't probably lost their lives fighting for a cause they believed in. We all believed in it.'

Seventy-seven-year-old Chiman now spends most of his time farming. Occasionally, he goes to the public village pool for a swim. Sometimes, he dives. And sometimes his old comrade Cdr Kapil V.P., who has retired from the navy and is settled in Noida, drops by. The two friends sit down with a bottle of Old Monk and get nostalgic about the old days when Bangladesh had not been born and they were just twenty-seven. 'I have three large pegs every day, but on days like that I don't count my drinks,' Chiman Singh says with a twinkling smile.

The Confession

19 December 1971
0745 hours
B-24, Naraina, Delhi

Brigadier M.L. Khetarpal is in his dressing gown, shaving, when the bell rings. Running his razor along his foamy chin, he hears the soft scrape of his wife's slippers against the floor and her footsteps leading to the front door. The latch clicks and the door creaks open. There is a hushed conversation. He hears the distinct rustle of paper changing hands. And then a scream and a dull thud. His wife appears to have fallen down. His face still soapy, Brig. Khetarpal rushes out of the bathroom.

He finds Maheshwari Khetarpal collapsed on the floor and a postman at the door. In her hand there is a telegram. Gentle, soft-spoken Mukesh, the Khetarpals' younger son—barely twenty and a student of IIT Delhi—is home too. He also hears the noise and comes out of his room, still in his pyjamas. As Brig. Khetarpal bends down to assist his wife, Mukesh takes the piece of paper from his mother's loosely clasped fingers. Tears spring to his eyes as he reads the telegram and then wordlessly passes it on to his father. 'Deeply regret to inform your son IC 25067 Second Lt Arun Khetarpal reportedly killed in action sixteenth December. Please accept sincere condolences,' it says.

~

May 2020
Khetarpals's bungalow
Forest Lane, Ghitorni
Delhi

Fifty years have passed. Mukesh Khetarpal is now seventy years old, while his elder brother, Arun, who smiles rakishly from a portrait on the wall, dressed in army fatigues, is an eternal twenty-one. Mukesh points that out himself. 'I have aged but Arun never will,' he says, his eyes crinkling up at the corners as he smiles. He says he clearly remembers the cold Delhi winter of 1971 when he was studying in IIT Delhi and Arun's Young Officers course at Ahmednagar had been interrupted by the war. Arun was recalled to his unit like all the other officers, and he had taken a train to Delhi, travelling in the pantry car since he could not get a reservation at such short notice. He had carted along his beloved Java motorcycle, a gift from his dad. Since there were a few hours before he had to catch the Punjab Mail to Jammu, he had unloaded his bike at Delhi and decided to ride it home.

'I was home that day,' remembers Mukesh. 'Arun parked his bike and walked in, looking extremely handsome in his black Armoured Corps dungarees. I was so envious, particularly of his uniform. He was in the peak of his physical health, just as most young officers are after their intensive physical training, and he knew it. He had the lithe body of a panther, a confident prowl, and he was so extremely proud of his uniform, his regiment, his country that it showed.'

Arun had reluctantly handed over the keys of his beloved bike to Mukesh and told him to look after it. 'He told me to keep revving up the engine from time to time so that the battery did not cease,' says Mukesh, confessing that since he was the younger sibling he had always been irresponsible and depended upon his elder brother to bail him out of trouble, which Arun had uncomplainingly done all this while. 'That day, Arun took me aside for a serious chat. "Look here!" he said, frowning at me. "You need to start becoming more responsible now that I am going to war. And if something should happen to me you have to take care not just of Mom and Dad but also Lalaji (our grandfather, Mr Chaman Lal Khetarpal),"' Mukesh remembers. Arun had always been very attached to his grandfather and as a little boy would often put his head in Lalaji's lap and coax him to tell stories of Partition and the First World War. In fact, when Arun received his first salary, he had placed a cheque in his grandfather's hands, making the old man's eyes shine with pride. Mukesh had obediently nodded, pocketing the keys to the bike. 'We were so young then. I never once thought that Arun might not come back. For me, he was just going on an adventure.'

Arun had packed up his golf clubs and his Blue Patrol uniform, explaining to Mukesh that he planned to play golf in Lahore and that he would need his ceremonial dress to attend the dinner night that would surely be held after the war was won. The Khetarpals had an early dinner, and it was at the dining table that Mrs Khetarpal said to Arun those famous words that would become part of army folklore. Recounting to him how his father and grandfather had both fought in wars, she had said, '*Sher ki tarah ladna, Arun, qayar ki tarah wapis mat aana.*' Arun had looked into her eyes and smiled.

Later in the evening, Brig. Khetarpal had taken out his grey Standard Herald car and, giving a warm hug to Mukesh and his mother, Arun had got in. 'Mom stood at the doorway, waving him goodbye. She was very concerned about him, but she was also very sure that her son would live up to what was expected of him,' Mukesh recollects. Arun, sitting next to his father, had pushed his head out of the car window and saluted his mother as she fought back tears and the car sped out of the driveway.

Early December went by in a haze. 'We had an imported Hitachi transistor. We would carry it around and spend all our time listening to Radio Ceylon, which was reporting the war in detail. Sometimes the signal was good and sometimes we could hardly hear anything, but we all sat around with our ears glued to it,' Mukesh remembers. On the evening of 16 December, Radio Ceylon reported that a massive tank battle had happened in Shakargarh. 'We knew Arun's regiment was in that area and our hearts sank.

There was a dreadful stillness in the house all evening. In our hearts there was this terrible fear about Arun's well-being, but nobody wanted to say it out loud.' The very next morning, there came the announcement that Prime Minister Indira Gandhi had declared a ceasefire. The war had finally ended. 'It was such a relief to us,' Mukesh recollects. 'We started smiling and talking once again. My mother got Arun's room cleaned up and we started looking forward to the day he would be back home, recounting stories from the battlefield.'

And then, on 19 December, the bell rang, and his mother opened the door to the postman.

~

'That telegram shattered our lives forever,' remembers Mukesh. 'After that, a sadness seeped into our lives. My father, who was bursting with pride when Arun graduated from the Indian Military Academy and joined Poona Horse, was never the same again. He had so many dreams for Arun. But Arun left us all so suddenly. Both my parents never recovered from the loss. My mother immersed herself in household chores. Papa became quiet and withdrawn. He stopped going to the Delhi Gymkhana Club and meeting people, something that he used to love doing earlier. He would spend most of his time locked up in his room,' Mukesh remembers.

Thirty years passed as the Khetarpals slowly accepted their loss and came to terms with their grief. Mukesh studied at IIT Delhi, found a job, got married and had a daughter, though he continued to stay with his parents. And then one day, he and Mrs Khetarpal were surprised to see Brig. Khetarpal smiling again. He looked happy. 'He said he was going to Sargodha, his ancestral place in Pakistan where the family had lived before Partition,' says Mukesh. 'It had been his long-standing desire to revisit the place where he had spent the early years of his life, and he had now decided to go ahead and do it.' Both Mukesh and Mrs Khetarpal tried their best to dissuade Brig. Khetarpal, but he would not hear a word from them. '"You are eighty-one. Where will you go?" we asked him, but he dismissed all our pleas. "It is decided. I am going," he told us. "Don't argue with me."'

Brig. Khetarpal told them that an old-boys reunion had been planned at Government College, Lahore (where Brig. Khetarpal had studied as a young boy). He said he would be in Pakistan for three days and would take a taxi and make a day trip to Sargodha before returning to India. Mrs Khetarpal's worries about where he would stay were dispelled. 'I am staying with another graduate of our college, a Pakistan Army officer who lives in Lahore,' he told her. 'That reassured us a little, and finally, when the day arrived, we drove him to the airport, where he got on to the Air India flight and waved us a happy goodbye. He was as excited as a schoolboy,' says Mukesh.

Brig. Khetarpal called his family from Lahore. He told them that his host was a perfect gentleman who had come to receive him at the airport and was taking very good care of him. '"*Bahut badhiya log hain. Meri bahut achhi dekhbhaal kar rahe hain*," he told us,' reminisces Mukesh.

Three days later, it was time for Brig. Khetarpal to return, and Mukesh drove to the airport to pick up his father. He found in him none of the excitement with which he had gone. 'Papa appeared very quiet and withdrawn. When I asked him if he was well, he assured me he was. I just thought the trip had tired him out and told him to rest. Even at home he wouldn't talk to us about the visit, which surprised us. Once again, he stopped going out of the house, keeping to himself most of the time.'

A week later, the Khetarpals were visited by 1971 war veteran Maj. Gen. Ian Cardozo, who was releasing a book on Param Vir Chakra award winners. Since Arun's story was also in the book, he had come to invite Brig. and Mrs Khetarpal to the launch at the Ashok hotel. Brig. Khetarpal agreed, and both he and Mrs Khetarpal went to the function on the assigned date. After the event was over, Brig. Khetarpal was surrounded by reporters who wanted to ask him questions about Arun. A week later, Mukesh was reading *India Today* magazine when he came across an article that talked about his father's Pakistan trip and his meeting with the Armoured Corps officer who had been the cause of his son's death. A shocked Mukesh read it and then went looking for his father. 'I confronted him and asked if what I had read was true. He said it was. When my mother and I asked him why he had not shared this with us, he said what could he have told us. It was not a pleasant episode.' And that was when a shocked Mrs Khetarpal and Mukesh heard what had transpired in Lahore when Brig. Khetarpal had been a revered guest at Brig. Khwaja Mohammad Naser's house in Lahore.

~

1 March 2001
Lahore

Brig. Khetarpal dabs his mouth with a napkin and is pushing his chair back after having finished dinner when he catches his host's eye. The retired Brig. Khwaja Mohammad Naser, the Pakistan Army officer who has volunteered to be his host for the three-day Lahore stay, has a hesitant smile on his weather-beaten face. '*Mausam achha hai, brigadier sahab, Insha Allah kuchh der bahar bageeche mein chal kar baithen?*' he asks. It is day three of Brig. Khetarpal's Pakistan visit. He has just returned from Sargodha and is tired, but is also touched by the fact that Brig. Naser has gone out of his way to make the trip comfortable for him. On his request, the Pakistani officer had even organized a videographer to document his visit to his ancestral home. Ideally, he would have liked to get to his bedroom and sleep early, especially since he has a morning flight to Delhi, but being the perfect gentleman, he does not have the heart to refuse his host's request. He is overwhelmed by the love and respect shown to him by the entire household.

'*Kyun nahin!*' Brig. Khetarpal says, smiling back. '*Kal subah toh main nikal jaunga, phir aapse baat kahan ho payegi.*'

The gracious Brig. Naser opens the door to the veranda of his beautiful house and leads his guest outside, where easy chairs are laid out on the lawn.

Brig. Khetarpal is surprised to notice discomfort in the Pakistani officer's eyes. He is reminded of the compassionate glances he had found the ladies of the household exchanging at dinner time. Brig. Naser is looking at the grass. He looks up to find Brig. Khetarpal's eyes on him. '*Main kuchh qubool karna chahta hun, brigadier sahab*,' he says softly.

'*Kahiye, beta, main sun raha hun*,' Brig. Khetarpal replies, looking affectionately at his host, who is younger than him by around thirty years. Brig. Naser clears his throat. 'Sir, there is something I wanted to tell you for many years, but I could not get the opportunity,' he says. 'I too participated in the 1971 war. I was then a young major, squadron commander of the Pakistan Army's 13 Lancers,' he says. Brig. Khetarpal is surprised—13 Lancers is the same regiment which had exchanged its Sikh squadron with the Muslim squadron of Poona Horse (his son's regiment) during Partition in 1947. On 16 December 1971, in a sense, the Indian and Pakistani soldiers had fought their old regiments. 'We fought Poona Horse in the Battle of Basantar,' says Naser, 'Sir, I am the man who killed your son.' A speechless Brig. Khetarpal listens quietly.

'On the morning of 16 December 1971, I was leading the counter-attack of 13 Lancers against the Indian bridgehead at Basantar,' Brig. Naser recounts. 'Your son was on the opposite side, standing there like a rock. In the battle, tank casualties were high. He destroyed many of our tanks, and finally, it was just the two of us left facing each other with our tanks just 200 m apart.'

We both fired simultaneously, and both our tanks were hit. It was, however, destined that I was to live, and Arun was to die,' Naser says. 'Your son was a very brave man, sir. He was singularly responsible for our defeat.'

Stunned, Brig. Khetarpal can only ask, 'How did you know it was Arun's tank?'

Naser tells him that ceasefire was declared the next morning (17 December), and with that the war ended. When he went to collect the bodies of his dead comrades, his arm in a bandage from the injuries he had suffered in the battle, he also checked on his damaged tank. That was when he saw Indian soldiers trying to extricate the tank he had battled with a day before. Curious about the identity of the brave man who had fought him so fiercely, Naser walked up to the soldiers and inquired who had been commanding the tank. He was told it was 2nd Lt Arun Khetarpal of Poona Horse. '*Bahut bahaduri se lade aapke sahab. Chot toh nahi aayi unhe?*' he asked the soldiers. They told him that Arun was martyred on the battlefield. '*Sahab shaheed ho gaye.*' A crestfallen Naser returned to his tent.

Brig. Khetarpal is listening in complete silence. Naser tells him that he realized much later, when Arun got the Param Vir Chakra and became a national hero, how young he was. 'I didn't know he was only twenty-one, sir,' he says. 'We were both soldiers doing our duty for our nations. I salute your son for what he did. I salute you too because I now know where he received his values from.'

The two officers sit quietly under the moonlight for some time. Then Brig. Khetarpal slowly gets up from his chair. Naser springs to his feet as well. The two stand together in an awkward silence, the moon lighting up Naser's grief-ridden face. Brig. Khetarpal looks at his moist eyes and moves forward to gently hug the man who killed his son. He then crosses the lawn and walks back to his bedroom.

The next day, just before Brig. Khetarpal is to leave for the airport, photographs are taken. Brig. Naser escorts him to the airport and sees him off respectfully. Two weeks later, Brig. Khetarpal is reading the newspaper in his Delhi house when he gets a parcel. It has come from Pakistan and contains photographs of his Lahore visit. Among them is a picture of him and Brig. Naser standing next to each other. They are both dressed in dark suits. Brig. Naser has an arm around his honoured guest. Behind the picture is a handwritten note. It says:

> To, Brigadier M.L. Khetarpal, father of Shaheed Second Lieutenant Arun Khetarpal, PVC, who stood like an insurmountable rock, between victory and failure of the counterattack by the 'SPEARHEADS' 13 Lancers on 16 December 1971 in the battle of Bara Pind, as we call it, and Battle of Basantar, as 17 Poona Horse remembers.
>
> Brigadier Khwaja Mohammad Naser, 13 Lancers
> 2 March 2001, Lahore, Pakistan

~

The family never spoke about the meeting again, Mukesh says. 'It was a trigger for painful memories from the past to come back and haunt us.' Sometime later, Brig. Naser toured India as manager of the Pakistani hockey team. He wanted to meet the Khetarpals, but Mukesh says none of them encouraged it. 'The past was not a place that we wanted to revisit. We just wanted to forget what he had told my father and move on in life.'

Brig. Naser's confession might have broken Brig. Khetarpal's heart but when he was interviewed about it by *India Today* he appeared calm and composed. There was no rancour for Naser. 'I'm an old soldier, I know the feeling. It's a will to dominate on the field,' he said. 'Naser is a soldier and he was doing his duty towards his country.'

~

16 December 1971
Battle of Basantar

On the battlefield of Bara Pind, 40 km into Pakistan, 2nd Lt Arun Khetarpal is crouched inside the cramped interiors of Famagusta, his Centurion tank which is named after a port in Cyprus. He is watching the enemy tanks in front of him. Most of them are wrecked and burning, the flames filling the sky with billowing grey smoke. The dead, the dying, the wounded are lost in the screams of shells. Ten Pakistani tanks have been destroyed, of which Famagusta has smashed four. However, it too has been hit and is now on fire. Arun knows this. He has switched off the radio set because he is being asked to pull back. His gun is still firing. He knows changing his position will give the enemy an opening. He will not let that happen.

Tank driver Prayag Singh is pleading, 'Sahab, let's move back and douse the flames.' Khetarpal's face is as dark as the grey smoke emerging from the carcasses of Pakistani Pattons burning furiously on the battlefield. 'No!' he says, his voice cold and firm. 'We will not pull back an inch.' In his dark dungarees, gunner Nathu Singh takes position once again. In front of him the air is dark with fumes. Mingled with the heat from the flaming tanks is the stench of burning flesh. Right behind him stands his tall and handsome young commander, a dark stubble covering his gaunt face. He is shouting: 'On tank, Nathu.' Nathu Singh aims and fires. Arun is trying to judge the trajectory of the shot. He will know if it has hit home because the moment a tank is hit the Pakistanis raise their guns and run out. Their religion forbids them a death by burning. A vein is throbbing madly in Arun's neck. If he manages to get this one, his tally will be five. At that moment, the Pakistani Patton tank he has targeted fires back too.

There is a deadly whistling sound as a shell shoots in through the cupola of Arun's tank. The massive Centurion shudders. The loader's head is sliced off in a split second and Arun doesn't realize that the same shell has ripped his stomach. He is surprised when the confined interior of the tank fills with the acrid stench of burning flesh. By then the shell has smashed into his thigh. It has shattered the bone and bent his leg at an angle that traps it under the seat of his tank. Bleeding profusely and in intense pain, all he can whisper hoarsely to Nathu, who has managed to exit the tank and is trying to pull him out, is: 'I won't be able to do it.' With that, he closes his eyes for the last time.

The time is around 1015 hours. Arun Khetarpal, breathing his last, is only twenty-one.

Author's Note

On 17 December at 0830 hours, the guns fell silent. Indira Gandhi declared a unilateral ceasefire a day after the Pakistani Eastern Command had surrendered. Many brave soldiers had lost their lives by then. For their families, life would never be the same again.

This story is based on interviews with Mukesh Khetarpal and Sawar Nathu Singh. The Battle of Basantar excerpts have been taken from the book *The Brave*.

An Ode to the Unsung Soldier

11 December 1971
0430 hours
Rangewala
An enemy position in Pakistan, south-west of Ferozepur, Punjab

Twenty-four-year-old Capt. Dhan Singh Adhikari stands in the battlefield where his battalion has fought and won a bloody battle. The orange rays of the rising sun are seeping through the purple darkness of night, and in that faint glow he sees men who had been talking and laughing with him till a day back lying dead or dying, their blood spattered on the land, their hapless eyes staring into oblivion. The dynamic Maj. Yash Sehgal, company commander, Alfa Company, is lying face down, his lifeless fingers spread out in the mud. A soldier turns him over gently. Three bullets have gone through his chest. His shirt is smeared red. His open eyes are glassy, his mouth open in a snarl of pain. Adhikari bows his head in respect.

Just a little distance away lies Maj. Ram Rishi Yadav of Charlie Company, his handsome features stained by the blood slowly seeping out of a scalp wound, his helmet missing. His lips move. Adhikari kneels down and lowers his head but cannot understand a single word of what Yadav is trying to say. He lifts Yadav's blood-soaked head into his arms. In a few minutes, his dry, flaked lips stop moving and he is gone. Adhikari looks on, his eyes moist with unshed tears.

For the next two hours, the young officer—who has been sent to collect his battalion's war-wounded and dead—works with the soldiers, carrying casualties to a pre-decided safe spot. The men work relentlessly, their shirts spattered with blood, their hands gentle, their touch firm, their eyes full of grief. 15 Dogra has lost twenty-five young soldiers that night, including the company commanders of its attacking companies—Alfa and Charlie—both of whom have led from the front. Many more are seriously wounded. But the enemy post that had been occupied by Pakistan's 9 Baluch has been captured. Rangewala now has the tricolour fluttering in the early-morning breeze, though many of the braves who made that possible are no longer around to see it.

Once the post is secured, Adhikari is tasked to go to the nearby Border Security Force post to keep the enemy area there under surveillance. He washes his face and hands repeatedly, flushing the tears out of his eyes, changes into a clean uniform and climbs into a one-tonner truck that takes him to the BSF post at Gatte Hayat, which is a short distance away.

Notes from Captain Adhikari's Diary

The night of 11–12 December 1971
Gatte Hayat BSF post
Mamdot sector

Since no one could find any work for me in the battalion, I have been sent here and asked to keep the enemy area under surveillance. I sincerely tried to do that in the afternoon but nothing could be seen across the border. Finally, I returned to my bunker. The day has been long emotionally as well as physically draining. I am bone-tired and want to get some sleep. But the scene of death and destruction which I witnessed just a few hours earlier keeps flashing in front of my eyes repeatedly, as if on loop, and I lie awake haunted by horrifying memories of the morning.

Suddenly, around 2200 hours, a BSF jawan flashes a light in my face. '*Sahab, aapke liye call hai*,' he says urgently. I leap out of the bunker. My unit adjutant is on the line. He tells me to go and do a reconnaissance of Jalloke Duan, a nearby enemy position, the next night (12 December). Trying my best not to sound scared (which I am), I request him to send to me Lance Naiks Rajinder and Pritam (both from Alfa Company), who also happen to be my unit hockey teammates. I want them on my patrolling team. He mumbles a curt 'okay'. I sit there frozen with anxiety and fear, very sceptical about my own capabilities to perform the allotted task.

~

The night of 12–13 December
2200 hours

The sarkanda stalks rise six feet above the ground. They glisten in the moonlight and rustle as we walk, parting them with our hands and making our way through the sea of brown. Rajinder and Pritam had arrived early in the morning and are in remarkably good spirits despite having participated in the battle just a day before. I haven't slept at all and am tired and nervous, more so now that we have crossed the international border.

All three of us are carrying our personal weapons and two hand grenades each in our overcoat pockets. To remain light we have left behind our radio sets, water bottles, food and even extra ammunition. Taking turns to lead, we ensure that we hold each other's hands, lest any of us get lost in the dense wild grass. We literally crawl in the darkness, waiting every now and then to listen for any unusual sounds. When assured that our presence has not been detected by the enemy, we continue. Progress is painfully slow. Eventually, at about 0500 hours (on 13 December), we manage to come to the end of the sarkanda. Right ahead is an open patch. We see a few mud huts and an observation post from where an armed sentry is keeping watch.

Standing camouflaged in the grass, we watch the enemy soldiers who are barely 400 metres away. Some of them are talking and laughing. The enemy defences include open trenches and some covered bunkers. About 2 km behind them flows the Sutlej. We spend a few hours there, not realizing how fast the clock is ticking. Suddenly, around 1000 hours, the sentry spots us and shouts, '*Pakdo, pakdo*.' Half a dozen men in khaki emerge from one of the huts and start running towards us. Rajinder tells me and Pritam to run while he keeps the enemy at bay. Just as we are about to reach the IB, the enemy begins artillery shelling at us, but all three of us manage to return to the BSF post around 1155 hours, after spending nearly fourteen hours in enemy territory. Once we catch our breath, we quickly draw out a rough sketch of the enemy location. A debriefing is scheduled at 1600 hours for which the general officer commanding (GOC) Maj. Gen. O.S. Kalkat will personally be coming to the BSF post, I am told. The news surprises me since GOCs normally do not attend debriefings at forward locations.

~

Gatte Hayat BSF post
1600 hours

I stand nervously before a team of senior officers that include my commanding officer, Lt Col K.C. Tiwari, our brigade commander, Brig. P.N. Anand, and GOC Maj. Gen. Kalkat. After I finish my briefing, Gen. Kalkat expresses satisfaction with the recce and then drops a bombshell. He tells Col Tiwari that he wants me to lead an assault on Jalloke Duan and I should present the attack plan before him in an hour. I am stunned! I am one of the junior-most officers of the battalion with only two years of service; I haven't even completed my Young Officers course. I have no experience of commanding a rifle company, and now I am to be launched straight into battle without even knowing the men I am to lead. Since I have no choice, I draw out a shabby attack plan and at 1700 hours present it before the seniors.

Maj. Gen. Kalkat suggests some modifications. He tells me to take one additional platoon to carry out a 'block' behind the enemy position so that the enemy cannot escape across the Sutlej River. The attack is to be carried out the very next night (14–15 December) as the Indian Army is under pressure to declare ceasefire at the earliest. The GOC pats me on my back, wishes me luck and then leaves the location. I am a bundle of nerves. I request my CO to give me Alfa Company (which suffered the maximum casualties two nights earlier) and a platoon from Charlie Company for the attack. Both companies have lost their commanders but they had shown a brave face in battle, and I want to make the best of their battle experience.

The attack plan is clear. We are to sneak into enemy territory at 2200 hours and reach an imaginary FUP by midnight. Ensure the 'stop' platoon is at the river line by the same time. Carry out heavy bombardment on enemy locations for ten minutes and then charge on the first objective. Tanks are to cover our move from the FUP. Jalloke Duan is to be captured by 0200 hours, after which we are to advance to the river line, reorganize and send the code word 'adhikar', which means we have succeeded. I have no idea how it will get done, but the next morning when all the troops including the crew of all three tanks and artillery have assembled near the BSF post, I carry out a detailed briefing, trying to sound confident.

~

The night of 14–15 December
2100 hours

Alfa Company, one platoon of Charlie Company and I line up in a single file to cross the international border. Lance Naik Rajinder is leading us. Unfortunately, he gets disoriented in the sarkanda bushes and after about thirty minutes brings us back to the starting point. I then decide to lead the column myself. This time we do not get lost and manage to reach the FUP just in time.

At 1201 hours (15 December) I ask my forward artillery officer to bring on artillery fire on the enemy for ten minutes. The air is filled with fire and smoke as screaming shells start targeting enemy trenches and bunkers. Just as our artillery fire stops and we are preparing to charge, the enemy retaliates. Besides small arms, they are using LMGs, MMGs and RCL guns. The fire is so intense that instead of the planned charge, we are all lying flat on the ground, trying to save our own lives. Thankfully, it is all going over the sarkanda. Each time I look up, I see bullets whizzing over my head.

The worst, however, is yet to come. Soon, shells start landing all over the place, kicking up clouds of dust. Deadly shrapnel is flying everywhere, and the battlefield is lit up like it is daytime. I look for my men and find them all lying on the ground, scared and motionless, their heads buried in their arms. For nearly thirty minutes, I am completely lost and don't know what to do. All of a sudden, the enemy fire stops.

Just then, my radio operator, Lance Naik Kirpa Ram, who also happens to be our unit hockey team goalkeeper (used to directing players from the goal line), crawls up to me. '*Sahab, ab aage chalte hain. Main sabko uthata hun*,' he whispers in my ear. As soon as I get up, an LMG starts firing in our direction. A jawan carrying a rocket launcher springs up next to me and says, '*Sahab, main isse thokta hun*.' I tell him to go ahead, not expecting much. The jawan fires one round. And lo! The fire stops.

I get up and start moving towards the objective, not realizing that I am crossing a minefield laid by the enemy. Naik Rapho Ram of the medical platoon follows me along with six other men. We have barely gone 20 yards when there is an explosion. Rapho Ram has stepped on a mine that has blown up one of his feet. He collapses but soon drags himself to a sitting position. Though in intense pain, he looks me in the eye and bravely declares, '*Sahab, aap chalte raho*.' There is no time to lose. I continue and we manage to cross the minefield. Kirpa Ram goads the men who are still waiting on the other side by shouting at the top of his voice, '*Jaldi cross karo, ab hum objective par hain*.' The soldiers follow unquestioningly.

Jalloke Duan

Soon, the whole company is across the minefield. Due to lack of proper orders from me, all of them have bunched up together. If even one enemy shell lands on us, the whole company will be written off. Thankfully, that doesn't happen. At about 0115 hours, we start clearing enemy trenches and bunkers one by one. The night is dark and visibility is just about 10 metres, but despite that, by 0230 hours, we have captured all trenches on the right-hand side and recovered enemy weapons, rations and twelve pocket-sized Qurans, which we respectfully place in one of the huts.

Totally exhausted, I decide to take a break and tell the men to sit quietly in the captured trenches and await further orders. Suddenly, I see three men in khaki rushing towards us. One of them is carrying an MMG with the ammunition belt flung over his shoulder. Panting with the strain of that extra load, he asks, '*Kya yeh Delta Company hai*?' Naik Bhuri Lal, who is busy shovelling sand from the trench next to ours, saves our lives by immediately pouncing on the enemy soldier without a thought for his own safety and hits him hard with his shovel. The man collapses while the other two disappear into the darkness. From the injured man, we learn that 9 Baluch is the enemy unit in the location. Meanwhile, the enemy artillery recommences shelling about 200 yards in front of us and it continues till morning.

By 0630 hours, we manage to clear all enemy trenches and think Jalloke Duan has been captured. Just then, an

MMG starts firing bursts at us from the far left. Naib Subedar Mauji Ram, another jawan, and I rush towards that bunker. The jawan crawls up from one side and throws a grenade inside. Reacting instinctively, the enemy soldier picks up the grenade and throws it out. Before he can turn his barrel towards us, I leap forward and let go a burst from my Sten carbine, hitting him on the knee. Mauji Ram quickly overpowers him.

~

15 December 1971
0700 hours

The nine-hour battle has ended, and the area is under our control. The first thing I do is physically count my men. Not a single one is missing. I thank God. We have captured fifteen rifles, one RCL gun, three MMGs, three LMGs, a rocket launcher, 200 mine boxes, a whole lot of ammunition and other weapons and equipment. It is time to send the code word, which I do, wiping sweat off my brow even in the freezing cold of December.

~

September 2021
Devender Vihar
Gurugram

The handsome, grey-haired Brig. D.S. Adhikari (retd) is just back from playing a game of tennis and is being served a piping hot cup of tea by his beautiful, soft-spoken wife, Usha. Telling me about the attack that he led, he says he gives complete credit for the operation's success to his men. 'They were led into battle by an officer with no experience, with whom they had never interacted before, yet they followed every order I gave them. They reposed faith in me and kept prompting me throughout the battle. They understood my constraints and didn't let me down. We often forget to acknowledge the unflinching faith and loyalty of our troops, but the fact is they are our unsung heroes.'

The war veteran confesses that even though fifty years have gone by, he sometimes still wakes up in the middle of the night drenched in sweat, having dreamt and relived the trauma of that morning he was sent to collect casualties after the Battle of Rangewala. 'I was just twenty-four years old then, and that moment of horrifying loss can never be erased from my mind. The pain and sacrifice of my comrades shall be a part of my life as long as I am around. They laid down their lives for the paltan and the country,' he says.

Author's Note

The battalion 15 Dogra fought the battles of Rangewala and Jalloke Duan across the international border, west of Mamdot town, in December 1971. Capt. Adhikari was decorated with a Vir Chakra for the operation. He went on to command 11 Dogra. The captured territories were handed back to Pakistan after the Simla Agreement. Besides the losses they face in war, numerous soldiers suffer terrible psychological trauma nearly all their lives which usually goes unaccounted for.

Closure

March 2012
Jari village
Jharkhand

Lt Col Quazi Sajjad Ali Zahir, Bir Protik of the Bangladesh Army, waits outside the house of the late Lance Naik Albert Ekka, Param Vir Chakra. His striped blue cotton shirt is a little crushed, and his green trousers look rumpled. He has made a long journey from Dhaka with human rights activist and Bangladeshi journalist Shahriar Kabir. The two of them first took a flight to Calcutta, then a train to Ranchi, and finally, after a long taxi ride, they have reached Jari, the small village in Jharkhand where Balamdina Ekka, widow of the martyr who gave his life in the 1971 war, lives.

The door opens and a frail old lady steps out. Draped in an old white cotton sari with a red border, wearing red plastic bangles around her wrists, she walks with the help of a stick and slowly shuffles across to meet them. It has been forty-one years since her husband left her to fight a war from which he was destined never to return.

Balamdina Ekka peers into Sajjad's spectacled eyes. She has been told that a Bangali sahab is coming to see her. He is standing with his hands folded. '*Maaji, main Bangladesh se aaye hun*,' he says in broken Hindi. '*Lance Naik Albert Ekka ka balidaan humara desh aaj bhi yaad korta hai*.' Balamdina touches his face gently, as if caressing a long-lost son who has shown up after many years. She says something in Kuduk, the dialect spoken in the Chhotanagpur region, to her son, Vincent, who has followed her out. Vincent was just a year old when Albert went to war and has no memories of his father. Sajjad does not understand Balamdina's words but he can read the sadness in her faded eyes. She invites him inside.

'As we talked, with Vincent acting as interpreter, Balamdina told me she had heard about Bangladesh and Gangasagar, the place where her husband was martyred,' Col Sajjad tells me on a frequently interrupted long-distance phone call from Dhaka. 'I opened the album I had carried and showed her photographs of Gangasagar, the Pakistani defence positions and the location where her husband was killed. She touched the pictures with deep affection and held them close to her chest.'

For a long time, Balamdina looks at the pictures she has never seen before. She is finally getting to see where her husband fought his last battle. Slowly, tears start trickling down her wrinkled cheeks. Dabbing her eyes with the edge of her sari pallu, the old lady goes on to share with Sajjad her memories of December 1971, when some soldiers had come to visit her and gently broken the news of her husband's martyrdom.

Though she was really young at that time, Balamdina tells him that she has understood he had made a huge contribution to the battle. 'They said he saved the lives of his comrades,' she tells Sajjad, and he nods. She goes on to tell him that this is the first time someone has come to see her from Bangladesh, the country her husband gave up his life for. Sajjad holds her soft, wrinkled hand in his and explains how Albert contributed to the Battle of Gangasagar. He narrates the saga of Albert's last sacrifice, his sheer audacity in the face of the enemy as he moved, clearing one bunker after another, till his final foray into the railway signal building where he took on two enemy soldiers and silenced the MMG that had been raining death on his comrades. Vincent and Balamdina listen spellbound.

Gently, he tells the old lady sitting beside him with her eyes glued to his face how Albert was hit by enemy bullets and closed his eyes forever. Her sallow cheeks are moist with tears. 'Did he put up a good show? Did he die well?' she asks, looking for reassurance. 'He did, maaji,' Sajjad says. 'You should be proud of him.' Balamdina smiles through her tears. She tells him that she has always wanted to see the place where her husband died. Embarrassedly, she confesses that she gets a monthly pension of Rs 5000. Vincent's autorickshaw has broken down and they will not be able to afford the trip. 'I told her it would be my honour to take her to Gangasagar,' says Col Sajjad.

As dusk falls, Sajjad slowly withdraws his hand from the grip of Balamdina's fingers. He tells her he has to go. 'Stay one more day,' she pleads. He assures her he will return.

'*Main wapis aayega, maaji; abhi mujhe jaane do*,' he says. She lets him go. 'I did not want him to die so young and make Vincent an orphan,' she is mumbling to herself as she and Vincent walk Sajjad to his car. He leaves with her words still ringing in his ears and the realization that her sorrow and sense of loss had not lessened with time. 'I thought to myself, Albert Ekka, who fought and died for a cause greater than his own, was also a father and a husband, and while the memory of his sacrifice had dimmed with the passage of time, his absence was still felt every day by the ones who loved him the most,' says Col Sajjad.

On his way back, Sajjad stops near the statue of Albert Ekka in the town square and, after standing there in silence for a while, moves ahead. He returns to Dhaka, and as a member of a national committee to honour foreign nationals who have made a recognizable contribution to the 1971 war to liberate Bangladesh, he asks for Lance Naik Albert Ekka to be honoured with the Friends of Liberation War Honour. 'Bangladesh is harvested from the blood of many Ekkas,' he writes. 'As a country, we cannot forget that. Forty-one years have passed since Ekka's death, yet so few of us know of him and others like him. Death in performance of their duty brought blessedness to them. For their untimely deaths, each of their families has asked for so little. I feel we should undertake this task with humility, urgency and a profound sense of honour and gratitude for a human who sacrificed his life for our country. It is our duty as a nation to honour Albert Ekka and also to ensure that his wife, Balamdina, is able to visit Gangasagar for saying her much-desired prayer,' Sajjad writes further. The entire committee is moved by his narration. The recommendations are accepted.

~

22 October 2012
0600 hours
Dhaka

Col Sajjad has kept his promise. The Ekkas are in Dhaka. Balamdina has received the Friends of Liberation War Honour, but that is not her objective. More than once she has caught hold of Sajjad's arm and whispered to him, 'When are we going to Gangasagar?' He has assured her affectionately and patiently that her wish shall be fulfilled. That morning, he drives down to the five-star hotel where she and Vincent are staying. He has told the hotel staff very firmly that she is his mother and Vincent his brother. They have to be well taken care of. Since the two feel a little awkward in the posh hotel, Sajjad has requested the hotel to assign a woman attendant for the old lady and have meals served in the room. The previous day, he had personally asked Balamdina what she would like to eat. Some sabzi and rice, she tells him. Sajjad gently coaxes her to try some fish curry as well and she agrees.

That morning, the reception desk tells Sajjad that Mrs Ekka has been up all night. She has been pacing up and down and walking across to the reception attendant almost every hour to ask if the 'Bangali sahab' has arrived. Sajjad sees her pacing about, her face lined with worry. Her eyes light up when she sees him. 'Shall we go?' she asks. 'Yes, maaji! *Par pehle aap kuchh kha lijiye.*' She says she is fasting. She will eat only after she has prayed at her husband's grave. Sajjad escorts her to the vehicle waiting outside and sits at the back with her and Col Ashok Tara, Vir Chakra, also a company commander in the Battle of Gangasagar, who has escorted her to Dhaka. Vincent sits in front.

It is a tedious eight-hour journey over bad roads, but Balamdina appears lost in her own world; she is immune to the discomfort. Midway, Sajjad asks her if she would like a cup of tea and biscuits, but she declines. Around 1430 hours, the jeep reaches Gangasagar. It stops at the railway station where Albert Ekka had fought his last battle. 'Take me to the place where he died,' Balamdina says, her voice calm and authoritative. Sajjad and Vincent each hold one of her hands and support her in crossing the railway line. She shuffles along as fast as age will allow. There is anxiety on her face and nervousness in her eyes. She wants Sajjad to point out the exact spot where her husband gave his life. When Sajjad shows it to her, she kneels down and starts to pray. Villagers have started collecting around her. Among them are members of the Mukti Bahini, who were strong young boys in 1971 with a fire burning in their hearts but are now old and frail. They still have clear memories of the battle. They have seen the genocide, the killings, the sacrifice. They know who Albert Ekka was, and they understand the pain of the old lady who sits there on her knees with her eyes shut. They know she is praying for the husband who left her with a one-year-old baby and never returned to watch him grow, whose absence she has felt every single day in the last four decades of her life, spent alone.

Suddenly, Balamdina falls to the ground. She has fainted. Sajjad picks her up easily since she hardly weighs anything. He carries her to the station master's room and splashes water on her face. She opens her eyes. By then the villagers have started lining up outside. Some have brought her gifts. 'They started trooping in with fruits, coconuts, cow's milk, etc.,' Col Sajjad remembers. Balamdina acknowledges their affection graciously and then gets up and says she is ready to leave. 'She started talking and smiling. She was a changed woman,' Col Sajjad says. 'Her mind seemed to have found peace after she prayed for her dead husband. She believed he was finally at rest.'

On the way back, in the jeep, Balamdina places her frail hand on Sajjad's head and tells him with great affection, '*Tum achha aadmi hai.*' She calls him her '*bada beta*', the son Bangladesh gave her. The next day, a cheerful Balamdina thanks everyone for fulfilling her wish and leaves for India. At Agartala, she tells reporters in her native Kuduk that she is at peace. 'I can see my Albert everywhere,' she says, smiling happily. 'He is in the hills, the lake, the temple.' She has found closure.

Balamdina Ekka passed away in her village in 2021, exactly fifty years after she lost her husband. She was eighty-nine years old.

Albert Ekka

3 December 1971
0200 hours
Gangasagar
East Pakistan

Lance Naik Albert Ekka is sprawled on the ground. Around him the swamp bubbles. His boots are caked in mud, and he can feel an ant crawling across his leg. Ekka does not move an inch; ants are the least of his worries. Something drips down his neck, and, shifting his rifle to his left hand, he touches the wetness with the right. It feels too sticky for sweat. He brings his hand to his nose and is not surprised to smell blood. The bullet has caught him in the neck. Wiping his palm on his pants, Ekka grips his gun again.

It is going to be first light soon. He can tell even before he notices the faint orange glow in the eastern sky. He is an Adivasi and these things come instinctively to him. He breaks into a snake crawl. The bullet lodged in his arm is causing a shooting pain in his arm. The one in the neck is sending a thin trickle of blood that is dripping on to his shirt. The wound is still warm and isn't hurting yet, but Ekka knows it is just a matter of time before the blood loss and pain get to him. Putting his weight on his elbows, rifle in hand, he crawls into the darkness. He is making his way to the old double-storey railway signal building from where the devastating enemy MMG is emanating.

~

Ekka has reached the building. Each time there is MMG fire, the ground shakes under his feet. The night rings out with the cries of his own comrades, helpless before the MMG's killer accuracy and range. He knows that for his unit's attack to succeed, the enemy MMG will have to be silenced. Slinging his rifle across his back, Ekka climbs up the rusty old iron ladder leaning against the building. Reaching for a grenade, he removes the pin with his teeth and lobs it inside the old brick structure. Before the two enemy soldiers inside realize what has happened, the grenade explodes, making Ekka squint in the sudden burst of light and recoil from the splinters that have hit him in the stomach. It throws one of the soldiers against a wall and reduces him to a mass of flesh and blood. The other is unharmed and still bent over the MMG. Ekka jumps in from the window. Taking his rifle off his shoulder and with the gleaming blade of the bayonet pointing forward, he charges at the soldier operating the machine gun and pushes the blade into his stomach. Pulling it out with all his depleting strength, Ekka plunges the bayonet back into the man's chest. The MMG is still smoking when he wipes the dead man's blood off his face and stands there with the bloodied weapon in his hands. In his eyes there is extreme exhaustion.

~

Everything comes to a standstill as soon as the MMG falls silent. The night is suddenly quiet. And then the battle slowly starts turning in favour of the Indian Army. Maj. O.P. Kohli, company commander, Bravo Company, 32 Guards (later renamed 14 Guards), has watched Albert Ekka lob the grenade and climb into the signal station. His heart fills with pride at what his boy has done. He is relieved to see Ekka emerge from the window and start climbing down the ladder, but his relief does not last long. Midway, Ekka collapses and drops off the ladder. While the men of Bravo Company go about clearing bunkers, Lance Naik Albert Ekka, merely twenty-nine, lies almost lifeless under the iron ladder, laboriously breathing his last. He will never rise again.

Author's Note

Lance Naik Albert Ekka was the son of Julius and Mariam Ekka. He came from an Adivasi tribe in Ranchi and was a devout Christian. Eleven soldiers from 14 Guards lost their lives in the Battle of Gangasagar, while one officer, three JCOs and fifty-five other ranks were seriously injured. Twenty-five enemy soldiers were killed, while six were taken as POWs. The battalion was awarded three Sena Medals, one Vir Chakra and one Param Vir Chakra for the bravery of its men.

This story is based on multiple conversations, stretching over months, with Lt Col Quazi Sajjad Ali Zahir, Bir Protik, of the Bangladesh Army. The Battle of Gangasagar extracts have been taken from the book *The Brave*. Sajjad was twenty-one years old and serving with the Pakistan Army when he defected and crossed over to India to fight Bangladesh's liberation war. He was given the death sentence for deserting the Pakistan Army, which he still carries against his name.

Appendix: The Missing Fifty-Four

In the euphoria of war victories, we tend to forget the men in uniform who were lost in battle. Given up as 'missing in action' or 'prisoners of war', they disappear from public memory. Here is a list of soldiers who disappeared into enemy territory and were given up as missing in the wars of 1965 and 1971. For their families, the war never ended.

1. IC 12712 Maj. S.P.S. Waraich, 15 Punjab
2. IC 14590 Maj. Kanwaljit Singh, 15 Punjab
3. IC 14457 Maj. J.S. Malik, 8 Raj. Rif.
4. IC 23148 Capt. Kalyan Singh Rathod, 5 Assam
5. IC 23283 Capt. Giriraj Singh, 5 Assam
6. SS 23957 2/Lt S.M. Sabharwal, 87 Lt Regt
7. IC 19294 Capt. Kamal Bakshi, 5 Sikh
8. SS 22490 2/Lt Paras Ram Sharma, 5/8 GR
9. IC 20230 Maj. S.C. Guleri, 9 Jat
10. IC 18790 Maj. Ashok Kumar Ghosh, 15 Rajput
11. SS 19807 Maj. Ashok Kumar Suri, 5 Assam
12. Sqn Ldr Mahinder Kumar Jain
13. Flt Lt Sudhir Kumar Goswami

14. Naval Pilot CO Ashok Roy
15. Flt Lt Harvinder Singh (9441) F(P)
16. FO Sudhir Tyagi (Lo871) F(P)
17. Flt Lt Vijay Vasant Tambay (7662) F(P)
18. Flt Lt Lloyd Moses Sasoon (7419) F(P)
19. Flt Lt Ram Metharam Advani (7812) F(N)
20. Flt Lt Nagaswami Shankar (9773) F(P)
21. Flt Lt SC Sandal (8659) F(P)
22. Flt Lt Kushalpal Singh Nanda (7819) F(N)
23. Wg Cdr (4657) Hersern Singh Gill
24. Flt Lt (8160) Tanmaya Singh Dandoss/Dandass
25. Capt. (SS 20095) Ravinder Kaura
26. Sqn Ldr (5006) Jal Manekshaw Mistry
27. Flt Lt (8404) Ramesh Gulabrao Kadam
28. FO (10575) Krishan Lakhimal Malkani
29. Flt Lt (5105) Babul Guha
30. LNk (682211303) Hazoora Singh
31. Sqn Ldr Jatinder Das Kumar (4890)
32. Flt Lt Gurdev Singh Rai (9015)
33. Flt Lt Ashok Balwant Dhavale (9030)
34. Flt Lt Srikant Chandrakant Mahajan (10239)
35. FO Kathiezth Puthiyavettil Murlidharan (10575)
36. Capt. Vashisht Nath
37. LNk Jagdish Raj
38. Sepoy/Gnr Madan Mohan
39. Sepoy/Gnr Pal Singh
40. Sepoy Daler/Dilar Singh
41. SS 22536 Capt. Om Prakash Dalal
42. EC 58589 2/Lt Vijay Kumar Azad

43. JC 59 Sub Kali Das
44. JC 41339 Subedar Assa Singh
45. 2459087 Sep. Jagir Singh
46. No. 13719586 Lance Havaldar Krishan Lal
47. No. 1146819 Gnr Sujan Singh
48. Flt Lt Manohar Purohit
49. Pilot Officer Tejinder Singh Sethi
50. Sqn Ldr Devaprashad Chatterjee
51. Gnr Shyam Singh
52. LNk Balbir Singh
53. Gnr Gyan Chand
54. Sepoy B.S. Chauhan

Acknowledgements

I would like to thank:

All the 1971 war veterans from the Indian Army, Navy and Air Force, and from the Bangladesh Army, who gave me time for interviews and shared with me their fascinating war experiences, many of which translated into stories for this book.

Jaya Harolikar, wife of the late Brig. Arun Bhimrao Harolikar, MVC, for so generously giving me access to his war albums; and my friend Madhuri Katekar, for volunteering to go across to her house in Pune and sending me scanned versions of some rare and precious images, which you can see in this book.

Col M.M. Malik (retd) and Maj. Rajesh Singh Sahrawat (retd) of 4/5 GR, for meticulously going through multiple drafts of my story on the Battle of Atgram, to ensure that it was as factually correct as possible.

Maj. Gen. J. Manavalan and Brig. M.K. Ajith Kumar, for their constant and patient guidance through the writing of this book. Capt. (Indian Navy) B.S. Negi, for suggesting stories from the Indian Navy and putting me in touch with Petty Officer Chiman Singh, MVC. Sqn Ldr Puneet Pareek (retd), for helping me recreate the air battles of 1971 and painstakingly introducing me to the procedures and technicalities of air battles which were used in Flt Lt Vijay Vasant Tambay's last mission to strike Shorkot Road, from which he never returned.

My brother Col Sameer Singh Bisht, SM, for hand-holding me through the entire project, for finding stories for me, connecting me to people, reading drafts and brutally telling me to redo the ones he felt did not do justice to their heroes.

My St John's College (Agra) classmates: Lt Col Satyendra Verma (retd), for patiently reading every single chapter, often at very short notice, and making valuable suggestions that added substance to the initial drafts. And class topper Shankha Mukherjee, for translating into Bangla the conversations quoted in the story 'Behind Enemy Lines', which gave it so much local flavour.

My editor Gurveen Chadha, for her constant support and reassuring presence by my side at all times; publisher Milee Ashwarya, for being the rock-solid support behind every book I do; Vineet Gill, for editorial guidance; Penguin design head, Ahlawat Gunjan, for his brilliant visualization of the book cover; and artist Amit Srivastava, for his stunning cover painting that, for me, is a depiction of a twenty-one-year-old Lance Hav. Dil Bahadur Chhetri as I imagined him in the Battle of Atgram, with ferocity on his face and a bloody khukri in his hand.

The books *Missing in Action: The Prisoners Who Never Came Back* by Chander Suta Dogra; *Death Wasn't Painful: Stories of Indian Fighter Pilots from the 1971 War* by Wg Cdr Dhirendra S. Jafa; and *Operation X: The Untold Story of India's Covert Naval War in East Pakistan* by Capt. M.N.R Sawant, MVC, and Sandeep Unnithan, which helped me in understanding the backgrounds of the stories 'Missing', 'Jangi Quadi' and 'Behind Enemy Lines'.

And last but not the least, Hukum, for taking dog naps on the rug by my side through all the months that it took me to write the book. Each time I turned to him for reassurance, he would wag his tail in approval, without, of course, bothering to read any of the drafts.